William A. Tilden

A Short History of the Progress of Scientific Chemistry in Our Own Times

William A. Tilden

A Short History of the Progress of Scientific Chemistry in Our Own Times

ISBN/EAN: 9783337321703

Printed in Europe, USA, Canada, Australia, Japan

Cover: Foto ©ninafisch / pixelio.de

More available books at **www.hansebooks.com**

A SHORT HISTORY

OF THE PROGRESS OF

SCIENTIFIC CHEMISTRY

IN OUR OWN TIMES

BY

WILLIAM A. TILDEN,
D.Sc. LOND., D.Sc. DUB., F.R.S.

FELLOW OF THE UNIVERSITY OF LONDON
PROFESSOR OF CHEMISTRY IN THE ROYAL COLLEGE OF
SCIENCE, LONDON

LONGMANS, GREEN, AND CO.
39 PATERNOSTER ROW, LONDON
NEW YORK AND BOMBAY
1899

All rights reserved

PREFACE

IT fell to my lot, in the spring of last year, to be called upon to deliver one of the courses of "Lectures to Working Men" which have been given by the Professors of the Royal School of Mines and the Royal College of Science annually for the last five-and-thirty years. The celebration of the sixtieth year of the Queen's reign had taken place a few months previously, and it occurred to me that it would be appropriate to the occasion to attempt a survey of the progress made in the science and practice of chemistry during the preceding sixty years. The difficulty of the task lay chiefly in making such a selection from the immense range of material which at once presented itself to the mind, as to give to the audience a tolerably clear view of those discoveries which may be regarded as fundamentally important, without creating confusion by the introduction of too much detail.

It is obvious that, in the time at my disposal in six lectures, it was not possible to do more than sketch in very broad outline the general features of each subject, and the extent of progress which has been made in each direction. I was desirous of assisting my audience, most of whom, I believe I was justified in assuming, possessed at least an elementary knowledge of physical science, by referring them to some book by the aid of which they could verify and amplify such notes as they had been able to take of the lectures. But I could find no single book of moderate size which afforded a historical survey of the succession of events which has led up to the system of theory in chemistry accepted at the present day.

In the following pages I have endeavoured to provide for the student such information as will enable him to understand clearly how the system of chemistry as it now is arose out of the previous order of things; and for the general reader, who is not a systematic student, but who possesses a slight acquaintance with the elementary facts of the subject, a survey of the progress of chemistry as a branch of science during the period covered by the lives of those chemists, a few of whom only remain among us, who were young when Queen Victoria came to the throne.

If justification in a more strictly chemical sense were required for beginning such a story with the year 1837 or thereabout, it would be provided by recalling the fact that at this time the influence of

Liebig's teaching was beginning to be felt. The new organic chemistry and the system of practical instruction in research inaugurated by Liebig, were attracting students from every part of Europe.

A large proportion of the progress in discovery, which has gone forward with increasing rapidity since that time, may be attributed to the spirit they there and then imbibed, and which continued to animate so many of them when afterwards they were called as teachers to other schools.

A retrospect over so long a period as sixty years necessarily includes the consideration of the claims of many workers to a place among the founders of our science. It is not always possible, however, to determine exactly how new ideas originated, or to assign to every contributor to their establishment or overthrow his just share of credit. With reference to this matter, all I can say is that I have used my best judgment upon the recorded evidence, and I have endeavoured in all cases to be completely impartial. My own recollections carry me back over more than half the period referred to, and I am therefore in a position to speak with direct knowledge of some of the subjects concerning which, in times to come, uncertainty would be likely to arise.

Finally, I desire to point out that this does not profess to be a text-book giving a complete picture of the state of knowledge and of theory at the moment. Its object, as already stated, is to show by what principal roads we have arrived at the present position, in regard to questions of general and fundamental importance.

ROYAL COLLEGE OF SCIENCE,
    LONDON, 1899.

CONTENTS

	PAGE
PREFACE	V
INTRODUCTION	1

CHAPTER I

MATTER AND ENERGY . . 17

CHAPTER II

THE CHEMICAL ELEMENTS: THEIR DISTRIBUTION IN NATURE, AND RECOGNITION BY THE CHEMIST . . 37

CHAPTER III

RECTIFICATION AND STANDARDISATION OF ATOMIC WEIGHTS   60

CHAPTER IV

NUMERICAL RELATIONS AMONG THE ATOMIC WEIGHTS: CLASSIFICATION OF THE ELEMENTS 83

CHAPTER V

ORIGIN AND DEVELOPMENT OF THE IDEAS OF VALENCY AND THE LINKING OF ATOMS 108

CHAPTER VI

THE DEVELOPMENT OF SYNTHETICAL CHEMISTRY . . 144

CHAPTER VII

THE ORIGIN OF STEREO-CHEMISTRY—CONSTITUTIONAL FORMULÆ IN SPACE 181

CHAPTER VIII

ELECTRICITY AND CHEMICAL AFFINITY . . . 209

CHAPTER IX

DISCOVERIES RELATING TO THE LIQUEFACTION OF GASES . 238

CHAPTER X

SUMMARY AND CONCLUSION 258

INDEX 271

A SHORT HISTORY OF THE
PROGRESS OF SCIENTIFIC CHEMISTRY

INTRODUCTION

WHEN the French revolutionaries in 1792 determined that the dead past might bury its dead, that for them the world should begin over again with a new calendar and the year 1, a new era was indeed about to commence, though in a fashion and with results which they little dreamed of. Lavoisier's head fell to the blade of the guillotine, but there remained active minds among the chemists in France and England, and the time was near at hand when the consequences of their discoveries would prove to be more momentous than even that great convulsion which changed so much in France and other countries of Europe. Looking back a century, it is easy to see the general features of a social state wholly different from that which prevails in all civilised countries at the present day. And it would be no exaggeration to say that the greater part of the changes, advantageous to rich and poor alike, which have accrued in the course of this hundred years, arose directly or indirectly out of the discoveries in physical science, the full tide of which set in with the opening of the nineteenth century. Even the progress in biological knowledge, and the study of the relations of man to his surroundings, may fairly be counted among the consequences of the intellectual activity promoted and stimulated by the successful physical and chemical investigations of this period. Some testimony as to the recognition in our own time of the idea that the world in relation to science was then passing from the old to a new order of things, is to be found in the fact that the Royal Society, the oldest of the scientific societies in Great Britain, and one of the oldest in the world, commences its great "Catalogue of Scientific Papers" with the year 1800. Previously to this time, the only branch of science, apart from pure mathematics, which may be said to have made substantial progress was astronomy; and even in that case, while the mechanism of the heavens was pretty well known, observers had yet to wait half a century longer for that wonderful instrument the spectroscope, which would inform them as to the composition as well as the movements of the heavenly bodies. In mechanics, again, much was known as to the theory of the mechanical powers—the theory of latent heat and its application to the steam-engine, the pressure of the atmosphere and the use of the barometer—but the properties of gases in relation to temperature, and the phenomena of gaseous diffusion, were yet to be discovered, and the doctrine of the conservation of energy, one of the really great discoveries of our age, had yet to be recognised and established.

Electricity was in its cradle in 1800, and as to chemistry, the composition of air and water, and the general characters of acids, bases, salts, and the composition of a few minerals, were matters of knowledge so recently acquired, that they had hardly become familiar enough to be fully realised. The doctrine of phlogiston was, of course, by this time defunct, and Davy, Dalton, Gay-Lussac, Berthollet, and Berzelius were hard at work in their several countries erecting the system of chemical theory which lasted almost down to our own time, and of which the essential features have subsequently been developed, not abandoned.

The object and chief business of scientific chemistry has always been to find out what things are made of, to study their properties, and to discover the relation of composition to properties. But scientific chemistry did not begin till the middle of the seventeenth century, and its founder was an Englishman, Robert Boyle. Previously, what was called chemistry, or alchemy, was mainly a confused mass of observation largely erroneous, and of hypothesis mainly groundless. Two objects had been set before the inquirer, one the production of gold from base metal, the other the production of a medicine to cure all disease, including old age. Those days are now long gone by, and all the substantial *practical* advances and inventions of modern times may be said to have arisen out of the adoption of a new principle, the pursuit of knowledge for its own sake. The cultivation of exact observation of nature, the practice of experiment (which is the substitution of prearranged for natural conditions), and the use of common sense in the construction of theories, these are the steps which have led to real progress, to a better knowledge by man of his relation to the universe in which he is placed, and the adaptation of the forces of nature to his needs and desires.

The study of chemistry leads us at once to a classification of the materials of which the world, with its atmosphere, ocean, and inhabitants, animal and vegetable, are composed. We recognise, first, two great divisions in these materials, viz. simple or single stuffs, and compound. From the former we can extract only one sort of substance, and this we call an element. From iron, for example, we can get only iron, while iron rust is a compound, because we can get from it both iron and oxygen.

Observation of this kind, however, to be complete, must be not only qualitative but quantitative. We must know whether the compound, recognised by a certain association of qualities which distinguishes it from all other kinds of matter, is invariably composed of the same materials united in the same proportion. This has been done for us in a very large number of cases, and the proposition that a given compound is definite in its nature, and always contains the same ingredients combined in the same proportions, is a recognised principle which, though many times threatened, survives triumphant. To take an example, water is a common substance obtainable from many natural sources, and exhibiting variations of colour, density, and so forth. But these variations are only apparent, and are really due to the presence of other things mixed with it. It is most pure as it falls from the sky, but even then it brings with it gases from the air. When it falls upon the ground it meets with salts which dissolve, and which, when accumulated in quantity as in sea-water, give it a taste; or it may dissolve vegetable remains and become green, brown, yellow, according to circumstances. Pure water can also be formed by the chemist by uniting together hydrogen and oxygen gases, as first shown by Cavendish in 1784, and in other ways. But when separated from everything else—not an easy matter, but still possible—we know water as a nearly colourless[1] liquid, which crystallises into a solid at 0° C. (= 32° F.), and boils at 100° C. (= 212° F.), under ordinary atmospheric pressure. It is always composed of eight[2] parts of oxygen to one part of hydrogen by weight, or one part of oxygen to two parts of hydrogen by measure, and this admits of no variation whatever.

It follows from all this that the idea of the *indestructibility of matter* is taken as an axiom. The mass of a compound is the sum of the masses of

---

[1] It has a blue colour when seen in mass.
[2] The exact ratio is 15·88 to 2 or 7·99 to 1.

the elements which enter into it, and though a substance may change its form, it is never diminished in amount. From a series of chemical transformations a given element may be extracted at any stage, possessing the same properties and having the same weight as at first. This was probably a hard thing to believe and understand before the days when the materiality of gases (gas = geist = spirit) had been established, and practical methods for the management and manipulation of such light and bulky stuff had been introduced.

Chemists have been industriously testing all sorts of materials: the minerals which form the solid earth, the gases of the air, the waters of the ocean, and the strange, complex, and multitudinous forms of matter which make up the bones and muscles, the blood and nerves of animals, and the wood, pulp, and juices of vegetables; and out of this highly diversified mass they have extracted, not an infinite number, but a strictly limited and comparatively small number of simple things. In 1837, the year from which our story must commence, fifty-four elements were known. A question at once arises: If definite compound substances have a fixed composition, the elements in them being always present in the same proportion, what will be the consequence of bringing together two or three elements and making them unite? Will the same elements in the same proportion always produce the same compound? The answer is that this is not always so. The same elements combined in exactly the same proportions may produce two or more entirely different substances. For example, starch and cotton are both composed of carbon, hydrogen, and oxygen in the same proportions (C 44·44, H 6·17, O 49·38 per cent.), and the sugar of honey or fruit, and the lactic acid of sour milk, form another pair of compounds which contain the same ingredients in the same proportion. But while starch forms a jelly with hot water, and is useful as a food, cotton is quite insoluble in water, and is indigestible; while grape sugar is crystalline, sweet, and neutral, lactic acid is liquid, sour, and strongly acid. Here is a phenomenon, then, which must be accounted for, not by the nature of the elements present, but by some other hypothesis.

The facts of definite combination and of multiple combination, where two elements are joined in several proportions to form a series of distinct compounds, were long ago accounted for by the atomic theory of Dalton. According to this doctrine, which has been the fundamental hypothesis of chemistry for nearly a century, chemical combination is due to the close approximation of the separate particles of the substances uniting. Dalton has expressed the whole idea very clearly in the following passage taken from his "Chemical Philosophy" (1808): "Chemical analysis and synthesis go no farther than to the separation of particles one from another, and to their reunion. No new creation or destruction of matter is within the reach of chemical agency.

We might as well attempt to introduce a new planet into the solar system, or to annihilate one already in existence, as to create or destroy a particle of hydrogen. All the changes we can produce, consist in separating particles that are in a state of cohesion or combination, and joining those that were previously at a distance."

If, then, two elements combining in the same proportion may produce two or more distinct compounds, this can only be explained, according to the atomic theory, by the assumption that the atoms in the different compounds are the same in number, but differently arranged. But why should atoms combine together at all? This has been, and probably will always remain, one of the fundamental but unsolved problems of chemistry. Two bodies at a distance from each other are drawn together with a force which is directly as the product of their masses, and inversely as the square of the distance between them. This is the cause of weight, in which the earth as the larger body seems to draw all things to it, though the action is always mutual. So also a magnet attracts iron and some other metals; a stick of glass or resin, which has been rubbed, attracts light bodies, such as a feather. In the last case, as in the others, the action is reciprocal, the glass attracting the feather and the feather the glass, and the cause of the attraction is said to be the charge of electricity which has been developed upon both bodies. But after all, every one of these cases of attraction is only a degree less obscure than that which we call "chemical affinity," which operates at distances so small as to be immeasurably beyond recognition by our senses, and even probably by any direct means of measurement which we can experimentally apply. For although we know the LAW of gravitation as already stated, and can make quantitative expressions of the *force* with which bodies are drawn together in the other cases, we can only make guesses as to the essential nature of gravitation, and of the attraction due to magnetism or to electrical induction. In the case of chemical affinity, we not only do not yet know why substances unite together, but there is at present no measure of the law as to the distance through which particles of uniting substances may act upon each other. Nevertheless, speculation has of course not been wanting, and among the several hypotheses concerning the nature of chemical affinity, none has attracted more attention, or shown signs of greater vitality, than the one attributing chemical combination to the existence upon the atoms of charges of electricity of opposite kinds, in virtue of which they unite to form more or less completely neutral products. This idea is derived mainly from the discoveries in connection with chemical decomposition by an electric current,—begun by Nicholson and Carlisle, when in 1800 they for the first time decomposed water into oxygen and hydrogen; continued by Davy, who discovered potassium and sodium by the same agency; employed by

Berzelius as the basis of his celebrated theory; and studied lastly and chiefly by Faraday, who enunciated the quantitative statements which are known as Faraday's laws of electrolysis. In the decomposition of compounds by the current, the elements range themselves under two classes, namely, those which in electrolysis go to the *anode*[1] or positive electrode, and those which appear at the *cathode* or negative electrode. The former of these two classes includes oxygen, chlorine, bromine, sulphur, and others which are called *negative* elements; and the latter includes hydrogen and the metals which are called *positive*. But while it is true that a strongly positive element unites with a strongly negative element to form a very stable combination, there are many facts which render very difficult the application of this electro-chemical hypothesis to all cases of chemical combination.

In 1837 the great Swedish chemist Berzelius was still living, and his views about the composition of salts and acids were still predominant. Lavoisier had taught that the compounds of oxygen with metals formed bases, while the compounds of oxygen with non-metals, such as sulphur, were acids. By union of a base with an acid a salt was formed. Thus sulphate of soda was composed of soda or oxide of sodium, and sulphuric acid or trioxide of sulphur. Later, when it was found that salts may be formed by

---

[1] These terms were introduced by Faraday, and are in common use.

the union of elements like chlorine with metals, the name halogen [1] was given to such elements by Berzelius, and two classes of salts, called respectively *haloid* and *amphid* salts, were recognised. But in each class the proximate constituents of the salt, that is, the sodium and chlorine of common salt, and the soda and sulphuric acid of sulphate of soda, were, according to the Berzelian classification, respectively electro-positive and electro-negative, and in the compound were united by electric attraction. Faraday before this time had definitely declared his belief in the identity of electricity and chemical affinity; and Daniell, in his well-known "Chemical Philosophy," published soon after this time, refers constantly to "current affinity" in describing the effects of the electric current.

Such, then, were in general terms the views commonly accepted in inorganic chemistry. Faraday having long abandoned the pursuit of pure chemistry, the most famous by far among English chemists was Thomas Graham, then Professor of Chemistry in University College ("The University of London"), to whom science is indebted for his discoveries in connection with gaseous and liquid diffusion, and for his advanced views on the constitution of such acids as phosphoric acid, which are now called polybasic.

At the beginning of the century Germany had few chemists, and none of the first rank. In 1837 Liebig was in the height of his fame. But this distinguished

[1] ἅλς m. sea-salt, or simply salt.

man, whose work and teaching were destined to have so great an influence on the scientific and industrial future of his own country, and so powerfully to stimulate the development of scientific chemistry in England, had been compelled in his own youth to seek the instruction he wanted in the laboratory of a French chemist. His first investigation was made under the direction of Gay-Lussac, and his first paper was published in the *Annales de Chimie et de Physique*. Liebig did much to point the way to the physiologist, the agriculturist, the manufacturer, in the practical application of chemistry to useful purposes; but the great work which he had achieved in 1837 was to inaugurate the systematisation of what was then rightly called *organic* chemistry, as distinguished from the chemistry of minerals, salts, and inorganic nature in general. Previously to his time the very composition, to say nothing of the "constitution" of such substances as alcohol, sugar, and the vegetable acids, was almost unknown. Various imperfect and difficult methods of analysis of such substances had been used successively by Lavoisier, by Gay-Lussac and Thénard, by Berzelius and others; but it was only after an investigation extending over seven or eight years that Liebig succeeded in devising the process which, in principle and with modifications relating only to details, is used in every laboratory for the same purpose at the present day. All the compounds in question contain carbon, associated with hydrogen, oxygen, nitrogen, sulphur or other elements, one or more of them; but the great majority contain carbon, hydrogen, and oxygen with or without nitrogen. When such a compound is burnt in excess of oxygen, or in contact with a substance which yields oxygen, the carbon is wholly converted into carbon dioxide, the hydrogen is converted into water, the nitrogen is set free. These products are easily collected and their weight determined, and inasmuch as the composition of carbon dioxide and water is accurately known, the proportion of carbon and hydrogen in the substance burnt is easily determined. The exact determination of the composition of a large number of compounds of organic origin, such as those already mentioned, and a study of some of their transformations and of the products obtainable from them by oxidation and otherwise, led to very important consequences; for in the end a definite system of organic chemistry was established, and this was based upon the idea that whereas inorganic compounds are formed of elements united together in different proportions, organic compounds were formed of groups of elements which were capable of passing from one combination to another, and of appearing as components of many distinct compounds, as though they were simple. And just as in inorganic chemistry there are metals and non-metals which stand in antithesis to each other, so there are organic "radicals," as these groups were called, some of which play the part of metals, others of elements like sulphur, chlorine, or oxygen. Organic chemistry, then, came to be regarded as the chemistry of compound "radicals."

Ideas of this kind, however, rarely receive general adoption immediately. It had already been shown by Gay-Lussac that cyanogen, a compound of carbon and nitrogen, habitually imitated the element chlorine in its combinations. But the establishment of the idea of compound radicles[1] and their relation to the properties of series of compounds was undoubtedly due to the investigation by Liebig and Wöhler into the compounds of benzoyl [$C_{14}H_6O_2$], existing in bitter-almond oil, in benzoic acid, and in the compounds immediately derivable from them. The propagation of this doctrine was, however, not left to the efforts of Liebig and Wöhler alone, for by 1837 Dumas in France had so fully adopted the idea, that in a communication made jointly with Liebig to the Academy of Sciences,[2] he announced formally his adhesion to the doctrine. In mineral chemistry, he says, the radicals are simple, in organic chemistry the radicals are compound: "*Voilà toute la différence.*"

Dumas himself, senior to Liebig by about three years, had made by this time very important discoveries. Of these the most striking, whether considered in reference to its influence on the progress of "organic" chemistry, or its relation to the electro-chemical theory of combination, is the discovery of the phenomenon of "substitution." The story goes

---

[1] This is the more usual modern form of this word.
[2] *Comptes Rendus*, v. 567 (23rd October 1837).

that attention was drawn to the action of chlorine upon wax, by the annoyance caused at a soirée at the Tuileries by the irritating fumes emitted by the candles, which burned with a smoky flame. It turned out on inquiry that the wax had been bleached by chlorine, and the fumes emitted on burning were due to hydrogen chloride. Researches undertaken by Dumas led to the discovery in 1834, that in contact with many organic compounds chlorine is capable of replacing hydrogen atom by atom, so that for every atom of hydrogen removed, an atom of chlorine takes its place. It may be easily imagined how distasteful such a discovery would be to Berzelius and the school of electro-chemists, involving as it does the idea that a negative element may be exchanged for a positive element, without a fundamental alteration in the chemical character of the resulting compound. That such is the case was not admitted without a controversy which extended over many years. It has long been known that the property displayed by chlorine is possessed by bromine, and under proper conditions by iodine, and even by compound groups, such as the radicle of nitric acid.

Such then was the general condition of knowledge relating to chemistry, and to those branches of science immediately connected with it, which had been established when Queen Victoria came to the throne. The position of science, however, will be better appreciated if it is remembered that at this date none of the special societies which exist for the cultivation of pure or applied chemistry and physics had come into existence.[1] The Royal Society of London (chartered by Charles II. in 1663) and the Royal Society of Edinburgh (founded 1783) were the only important Societies to which communications relating to discoveries in chemistry could be appropriately addressed in this country, and in the *Philosophical Transactions of the Royal Society of London* are to be found the greater part of the discoveries made by Davy and Faraday. But after the death of Davy in 1829 it seems probable that there was considerable justification for complaint as to mismanagement in the Royal Society, such as took shape in Babbage's "Reflections on the Decline of Science in England," published in 1830. This, however, was a state of things destined soon to pass away, for not only was Faraday at work at the Royal Institution, but in 1831 the British Association for the Advancement of Science started upon its prosperous career.

We may now proceed to trace the course of discovery in chemistry, but as this necessarily advanced upon several lines, which were in the beginning at any rate quite distinct from each other, it will be advantageous to follow these separately, taking one at a time.

[1] The Chemical Society of London was founded 1841; Pharmaceutical Society of Great Britain, 1841; Société Chimique de Paris, 1858; the Berlin Chemical Society, 1867; the Physical Society, 1874; American Chemical Society, 1876; the Society of Chemical Industry, 1881.

CHAPTER I

MATTER AND ENERGY

IT has already been pointed out in the Introduction that chemical changes are attended by transmutations in the form of matter, but never by any gain or loss in its amount. The doctrine of the conservation of matter teaches that ponderable things are indestructible, and that the amount of matter in the universe, so far as its conditions are yet known, is absolutely constant and invariable. Without this fundamental postulate no system of chemistry could exist, nor indeed could the present order of things endure. This was practically acknowledged so soon as the minds and the writings of chemists were freed from the influence of the old theory of phlogiston, and hence we may say that it was adopted from the time when Lavoisier's explanation of combustion was accepted.

A second equally important principle is, however, necessary, though its full recognition was delayed for another half-century. This is the doctrine which affirms the *indestructibility of energy;* but it required for its establishment the thought, observation, and experiment of many generations of men. Newton had, no doubt, clear views of his own upon the subject, and these received expression in his statement of the laws of motion; but the experimental work of Rumford and Davy upon the production of heat by friction, were required to prove that such a form of energy as heat is not matter, as had been previously supposed. Measurements of the correlation of heat and mechanical work were not made till forty years later, chiefly by Dr. James Prescott Joule, of Manchester. If the determination of the first precise quantitative relations be regarded as the best foundation of exact knowledge, and if, as we now believe, this kind of knowledge is essential to the formation of correct ideas concerning chemical changes, then the name of Joule deserves to be ranked along with those of Boyle, Lavoisier, and Dalton, who have successively, at different times, by different writers, and for different reasons, been invested with the title of Father or Founder of modern chemistry. Since the recognition of the fundamental idea that all chemical changes involve redistribution but no destruction of energy as well as of matter, and that the same matter associated with different amounts of energy assumes very different aspects and properties, the progress of chemistry has been more rapid than in any previous period.

It is, however, time that some explanation should be offered as to the modern use of the word *energy*, and its application in connection with chemistry as well as other departments of physical science. When hydrogen combines with oxygen in due proportions the sole material product is water; but another and very significant effect is produced during the act of combination, and that is the evolution of heat. This heat is communicated to the water formed and to the walls of the tube or other vessel in which the gases are brought together, and it is thus soon dissipated. But the amount of heat thus produced can be measured, and this is usually done by observation of the rise of temperature in a given quantity of water into which the heat is conveyed, or what comes to the same thing, the determination of the amount of water, the temperature of which is raised one degree from zero. That amount of heat which will raise the temperature of 1 'part' by weight of water, 1 degree is spoken of as 1 calorie or 1 unit of heat. The same result can be attained by observing other thermal effects, as, for example, by noting the amount of ice melted.

Now when 1 part by weight, say 1 gram[1] of hydrogen, is burned in oxygen, and the water formed is collected in the liquid state, the amount of heat evolved is sufficient to raise the temperature of about 34,000 grams of water 1°, or, in other words, 34,000 calories or units of heat are evolved. This includes a certain quantity of heat, about 5500 units, which

---

[1] Throughout the book weights and measures of the metric system and degrees of the Centigrade scale will be used.

is given out in the change of the water from the state of vapour, in which it is formed, to the state of liquid, in which it is collected. The amount of heat produced in this way is constant for unit weight of either hydrogen or oxygen, and whether combination takes place quickly, by exploding a mixture of the two gases in a strong vessel, or slowly, by burning one of the gases at a jet in an atmosphere of the other, or by bringing them together in the presence of spongy platinum which makes them combine, the amount of heat given out is always 34,000 calories per gram of hydrogen. From this we learn that when hydrogen combines with oxygen a definite quantity of something is lost by the elements, and passes out of them in the form of heat: this something is called energy. The water which has been formed may be made to yield up the hydrogen and oxygen which have combined for its formation, but this can only be brought about on condition that that energy is restored to the two elements. This result may be reached in several ways, as by the action of a high temperature, or by the use of an electric current, or indirectly by the use of chemical agents.

If a penny is rubbed hard upon a board it becomes heated, and it is said that by hammering a piece of cold iron a skilful blacksmith can make it even red hot. In both such cases a sense of fatigue in the arm is soon felt, and there is a consciousness that *work has been done.* If we substitute for human effort the falling of a weight, similar effects can be produced; but just as fatigue puts an end to the work done by the arm, so the fall from a higher to a lower level corresponds to work performed which cannot be repeated with the same mass until it is lifted up to its original height. The power of doing work, called in physical science *energy*, is capable of measurement, and may take many different forms. For example, the arm whose muscular strength may be used to heat a mass of metal by hammering or by rubbing, may be otherwise employed to turn the handle of a machine by which a coil of copper wire is made to rotate in the field of a magnet, and thus an electric current may be produced in the wire. The current flows so long as the work is being done, and it ceases immediately upon the cessation of the motion. Further, it is a familiar fact that when a current of electricity flows through an imperfect conductor electricity disappears, and the conductor becomes heated. An example of this is seen in the common incandescent electric lamp, in which a thread of carbon is heated till it gives out a brilliant light.

Observations of such a kind must, however, be supplemented by measurements of the amount of heat or of electricity produced when a given amount of work is done. The problem is to find a suitable unit of work, and this is provided by gravitation. The question is, first, what amount of work must be done in order to produce heat enough to raise the temperature of unit mass water one degree? and secondly, supposing the water allowed to cool down again, and the heat which passes from it made to do work, how much work will be done? Answers to these questions are supplied by the investigations made by Joule, and published in 1843 and following years. The results which are considered most trustworthy were obtained by the following process. The work done was the descent of a mass of lead from a certain measured height to a lower level, and the heat corresponding to this was generated by causing this weight in its descent to move a paddle working in a vessel containing a measured quantity of water, and provided with fixed projections within, so as to prevent the water from being whirled bodily round. The friction thus caused gave rise to heat, and so the temperature of the water was raised through a certain number of degrees which could be determined by delicate thermometers immersed in the water. By this means it was found, as the mean result of a number of successive concordant experiments, that the descent of a weight of 424 grams through a distance of 1 metre, or 1 gram falling 424 metres, generates heat enough to raise the temperature of 1 gram of water 1° C. The same facts may be expressed in English weights and measures, by saying that the fall of 772 lbs. through 1 foot, or of 1 lb. 772 feet, gives a rise of 1° Fahr. in 1 lb. of water. The numbers, 424 gram-metres or 772 foot-pounds, according to the system chosen, represent the *mechanical equivalent of heat*, and are often spoken of as Joule's equivalent, and represented for mathematical purposes by the letter J.[1]

Other methods have been used, both by Joule and others since his time, such for example as the measurement of the heat generated by the friction of two metallic surfaces upon each other under determined conditions, and with approximately the same result.

Bearing in mind, then, that a definite quantitative relation is now established between mechanical work performed and heat generated when the work is all expended in friction, and that the same relation can be traced whether the work is transformed directly into heat, or is first made to generate an electric current, which is afterwards converted into heat, it is obvious that heat is not a substance but a mechanical effect, and, as now universally believed, the effect of vibratory or other motion in the particles of the heated body (see Chap. X.). We may now return to the question involved in the phenomena of chemical combination and decomposition.

[1] The value of the mechanical equivalent given in the text applies to the short range of temperature, which was, of course, near to common air temperatures, employed in the experiments. The specific heat of water increases as the temperature is raised, and the value for higher temperatures would therefore be greater. Professor Osborne Reynolds has made an elaborate series of experiments, in which the work done in raising the temperature of water from freezing to boiling point has been determined. The mean value deduced from these experiments for this range of temperature is about 777, and this corresponds to a value slightly higher than Joule's, namely, 773·7 for 1° Fahr. at 60° Fahr.—*Phil. Trans.*, 1897, A.

It is clear, from what has already been said, that an element usually differs from a compound not only in containing only one form of matter, but in having a power of doing work; that is, a store of energy which is more or less dissipated and lost when the element enters into a state of chemical combination.[1] The process of separating an element or other substance from a compound in which it is held by chemical affinity is comparable with the operation of raising a weight. In each case work has to be expended from some source—human, animal, or mechanical power, the falling of water, the pressure of the wind, the rising of the tide, the heat of the sun, or the chemical process involved in the burning of coal. Hence, to revert to the case of water, which is formed when hydrogen and oxygen unite together, it must now be obvious that, to separate the united hydrogen and oxygen, work must be done equivalent at least to the heat generated in the act of combination.

An element, then, is matter combined with potential energy. This energy, by appropriate means, may be allowed to run down, either all at once or by stages, as for example in the case of sulphur, the burning of which in oxygen may be arranged to produce sulphur dioxide, SO_2, or sulphur trioxide,

---

[1] This is, of course, not true in those, not rare, but much less frequent cases in which "endothermic" compounds, such as carbon bisulphide, are formed, the production of which is attended by absorption of heat, and their decomposition therefore by evolution of heat.

SO_3. An element which has been separated from chemical combination with other elements may, however, in some cases be compelled to take up an additional store of energy. This change may often be accomplished by the application of heat. The product is spoken of as an "allotropic" modification, or simply as an *allotrope* of the element. If sulphur, for example, is melted, and the resulting liquid raised only a few degrees above the melting point of common sulphur, a new substance is formed which crystallises in rhombic prisms, having a different form and a different density from common sulphur, the crystals of which are rhombic octahedrons. Or by heating the liquefied sulphur still further, it may be obtained in the form of a plastic mass wholly devoid of crystalline structure. But both these modifications revert in time to the common kind, and the change is attended by evolution of heat. Similarly, red phosphorus may be got from common white phosphorus by heat, ozone from oxygen by electricity, graphite or the diamond from common charcoal, by dissolving it at a high temperature in melted iron, and allowing it to crystallise under pressure when cooling. In all these cases the same matter is concerned, but different amounts of energy are bound up with it, and different amounts of heat are therefore generated when equal quantities of the various allotropes of any one element enter into chemical combination. Thus, 1 gram of each of the three chief varieties of carbon burnt completely in oxygen give the following amounts of heat expressed in ordinary units:—

Diamond	7770
Graphite (natural)	7797
Graphite (from iron)	7762
Wood-charcoal	8080

The possibility of the conversion of one element into another, as, for example, the transmutation of silver into gold, is a question which even in these days, so remote from alchemical times, has not been entirely set aside. But although the idea that the elements may have had a common origin, or may contain common constituents, may be admitted as worthy of discussion, evidence of a direct kind for either of these propositions is absolutely wanting. Such considerations as have been brought into the discussion have been derived chiefly from a comparison of the atomic weights, which will form the subject of a later chapter.

The combination of hydrogen with oxygen is attended, as already stated, by the formation of a definite amount of water and the evolution of a definite amount of heat. The determination of the quantity of heat thus disengaged has occupied at different periods many of the most distinguished chemists, from the time of Lavoisier onwards. The experiments of Lavoisier were made with his celebrated ice calorimeter, and subsequent determinations, in which the heat of union was communicated to water, were made by Dulong, by Favre and

Silbermann, and by Andrews. The examination of other cases of combination have led to the establishment of the important general principle, that every chemical change, whether of combination or decomposition, is accompanied by the evolution of a definite amount of heat, which is the same as saying that a definite amount of energy, previously existent in the bodies concerned, becomes dissipated. This is the first principle of that department of science which is called "thermo-chemistry."

One of the first serious workers in this field was Dr. Thomas Andrews of Belfast, and though later experimenters have improved upon his methods and results, his name deserves to be remembered as a pioneer in this difficult department of experimental inquiry. One of the most important series of experiments carried out by Andrews relates to the heat developed during the combination of acids and bases in aqueous solution.[1] From these experiments he drew the conclusion that the heat developed during the union of acids and bases is determined by the base and not by the acid. In this he was mistaken, for it appears that the heat produced by the neutralisation of an acid by a base is an effect to which both contribute, though in proportions which depend upon their chemical nature, and are not yet determinable. One of his general laws,[2] which states that "an

[1] *Trans. R. Irish Academy*, 1841; reprinted in the volume of his collected "Scientific Papers."
[2] *British Association Report for* 1849, p. 69.

equivalent of the same base combined with different acids produces *nearly* the same quantity of heat," has been confirmed by later researches, and has been explained by a hypothesis, of which an account will be given in a later chapter. Andrews also made determinations of the heat produced in other chemical changes, including the amount of heat disengaged during the combination of various substances with oxygen and with chlorine.

About the same time thermo-chemical researches of considerable importance were being carried on by the Russian chemist Hermann·Hess. As the result of his experiments on the neutralisation of acids diluted with different proportions of water, he was led to the enunciation of the principle that the sum of the several amounts of heat evolved during the successive stages of a process are the same in whatever order they follow one another; in other words, the effect is dependent on the relation of the final to the initial state of the system, and not upon the intermediate stages. On neutralising an aqueous solution of ammonia with sulphuric acid containing one, two, three, and six proportions of water there is a different development of heat in each case; but by adding to the results found by experiment in the three last cases the quantity of heat evolved when the monohydrated acid combines with one, two, and five proportions of water, nearly the same value is obtained in each case. Andrews thought this principle correct but self-evident. It is, however, of such importance that its experimental verification was very desirable. By the application of this principle it is possible to calculate thermal changes which are not capable of direct experimental determination. The heat evolved by the formation of carbon monoxide, for example, cannot be ascertained by burning carbon in oxygen; but by observing the heat evolved in the production of carbon dioxide, and then determining the heat produced by the combustion of carbon monoxide itself, the difference between the two affords the number required. One part by weight of carbon burnt to carbon dioxide gas gives 7797 units of heat, but 2·33 parts of carbon monoxide gas, which contains the same quantity of carbon, gives 5607 units. Now, if the amount of heat given out when the first atom of oxygen unites with the carbon were the same as that produced by the second atom, the total amount of heat evolved when carbon burns into carbon dioxide would be 5607×2, or 11,214 units. But the actual amount observed is only 7797 units; the union of the first atom of oxygen forming carbon monoxide is attended by the evolution of 2190 units; the difference, 3417, therefore must represent the heat rendered latent when solid carbon is converted into the gaseous oxide.

Nearly all chemical changes are associated in a similar way with physical changes, and hence in the great majority of cases the interpretation of the results is encumbered with serious difficulties. This is the case even when all the products remain in the same state, gaseous, or liquid, or solid, as the materials employed, for there is usually a separation as well as a combination of atoms even in cases which appear most simple. The union of hydrogen with oxygen, for example, is not merely

$$H_2 + O = H_2O$$

but

$$2H_2 + O_2 = 2H_2O,$$

from which it appears that the oxygen molecule is divided in this process into two parts.

Since the days of Favre and Silbermann, of Andrews and of Hess, the problems presented by the thermal changes which accompany chemical changes have been studied in great detail by Professor Julius Thomsen in Copenhagen, and later by Professor Berthelot in Paris.

Thomsen's first memoir appeared in 1853, and from that date down to the time when more than thirty years later he completed his great work in four volumes, *Thermochemische Untersuchungen*, the author pursued without interruption the systematic investigation of which he had laid down the plan so long ago. In this work the phenomena of neutralisation are first investigated, the succeeding volumes being devoted to the determination of the heats of formation of the more important oxides, chlorides, hydrides of the non-metals, and then of the metals, the constitution of aqueous solutions, the heats of combustion of organic compounds, and the thermal phenomena attending isomeric change; in fact, a body of data is provided which relates to all kinds of chemical changes, and is available for the use of theory in every department of the subject.

M. Berthelot tells us that it was in 1864 that he began to study thermo-chemistry. In 1879 he brought out his treatise entitled *Essai de Mechanique Chimique, fondée sur la Thermochimie*. This work embodies the chief results of all his researches on the subject which had been from time to time communicated to the *Annales de Chimie et de Physique*, where they occupy more than two thousand pages. The author sets forth in his introduction the three propositions which he regards as fundamental. The first of these states that the heat disengaged in any reaction is a measure of the chemical and physical work accomplished in that reaction. The second affirms the dependence of the thermal change upon the relation of the final to the initial state of the system; it is in fact the principle established by Hess, as already explained. The third proposition was introduced by Berthelot himself, under the title of the "Principle of Maximum Work." This it will be well to state as nearly as possible in the words of the author himself, inasmuch as it has been the subject of very severe criticism.

"Every chemical change accomplished without the aid of external energy tends towards the production of a body or system of bodies which gives out the greatest amount of heat." As a corollary from this, he adds that "every chemical reaction which can be accomplished without the assistance of preliminary work, or of energy external to the system of bodies concerned, proceeds necessarily if it is attended by evolution of heat."[1]

Here is a doctrine at first sight attractive in no ordinary degree, and which, if established, would appear to account for much that would be otherwise obscure. But unfortunately it is expressed in terms which are far too general, and is manifestly in opposition to well-recognised facts. In the first place, "endothermic" compounds are sometimes formed spontaneously, and in most cases of combination which is attended by evolution of heat the process is retarded and ultimately stopped, unless the heat generated by the union of the first portions of substance is conducted away out of the system. Ammonia and hydrogen chloride, for example, unite at common temperatures to form solid sal-ammoniac, and in this process heat is evolved. The consequence is that until the whole is allowed to cool below the temperature at which it is known that sal-ammoniac is resolved into these two gases, a portion of the materials remain separate, notwithstanding that their

---

[1] "Tout changement chimique accompli sans l'intervention d'une énergie étrangère tend vers la production du corps ou du système de corps qui dégage le plus de chaleur." And as a corollary from this, "toute réaction chimique susceptible d'être accomplie sans le concours d'un travail préliminaire et en dehors de l'intervention d'une énergie étrangère à celle des corps presents dans le système, se produit nécessairement, si elle dégage de la chaleur."—*Essai*, vol. i., Introduction, xxix.

union would be attended by evolution of heat. The same kind of thing is true of all reversible reactions, that is, all chemical combinations which are prevented by rise of temperature and promoted by fall of temperature.

Nevertheless Berthelot's principle, if applied with due limitation, does seem to accord with a number of familiar facts. The displacement, for example, of iodine by bromine, and of bromine by chlorine, in the combinations of these elements with hydrogen and the metals, and their apparent order of affinity in such compounds, is in accordance with the thermal relations of these elements, as shown by the following statement of the heat produced by the combination of hydrogen with equivalent quantities of each of them:

Formula-weights in grams.		Calories.
$H + Cl + 4H_2O$	give	39320
$H + Br + 4H_2O$	,,	28380
$H + I + 4H_2O$	,,	13170

Similar relations may be noticed among the metals. In such a series as iron, copper, silver, mercury, for example, where the apparent affinities for chlorine or oxygen are manifested in the order in which they are written, on the one hand by the displacement by each one of those which follow it in the list, and on the other by the heat of formation of their salts, which stands in the same succession.

The chief object of quantitative thermo-chemical investigation is, according to Julius Thomsen,[1] the

[1] *Therm. Untersuchungen*, vol. i. 3.

establishment of dynamical laws relating to chemical processes; but how little progress towards this object has been at present accomplished is manifest from the brief sketch which alone it is possible to give in these pages. Notwithstanding the labours of half a century, thermo-chemistry remains for the most part a mass of experimental results, which still await interpretation. For, apart from the assistance which such results afford towards the establishment of the doctrine of the conservation of energy, it is plain that successive attempts at generalisation have been unsuccessful when considered in a strictly scientific sense.

One direction, indeed, in which the relation of heat to chemical affinity has been studied with much advantage, is in the examination of those reversible chemical changes which are commonly brought about by change of temperature. The term *dissociation*[1] was introduced by Sainte-Claire Deville, in 1857, to designate decompositions of this kind, and, though it was but slowly accepted by the chemical world, it has now become firmly embedded in the language of science.

So long ago as 1846 it was discovered by Grove[2] that water is decomposed into a mixture of oxygen and hydrogen by contact with intensely heated platinum. The experiment was afterwards repeated by Deville, who found that decomposition begins at a temperature of 960° to 1000°, but that it proceeds

---

[1] "De la dissociation ou décomposition spontanée des corps sous l'influence de la chaleur."—*Compt. Rend.*, xlv. 857.

[2] *Phil. Trans.* Bakerian Lecture for 1846.

to only a limited extent. If, however, any means be taken to separate the resulting gases from each other, the decomposition may be carried much further. Regnault found, for example, that steam passed over melted silver is decomposed more freely, apparently because the oxygen is absorbed by the melted silver, which gives it off again on solidifying. These effects are not due to any chemical action on the part of the metal, but are the result of the high temperature to which the vapour is exposed. Hydrogen and oxygen combine together completely at lower temperatures. Results so remarkable as these did not attract the attention they deserved till some years later, when the systematic study of vapour-densities led to the discovery that a large number of familiar compounds, commonly reputed stable, are decomposible at various temperatures in a similar manner. In each case the products of dissociation reunite on cooling, producing the original compound. Sulphuric acid, for example, converted into vapour is no longer sulphuric acid, but a mixture of vapours of water and sulphur trioxide, which on cooling reunite. By conducting the operation in a flask with a long drawn-out capillary neck, the water vapour, being the lighter of the two, diffuses away more rapidly, leaving a preponderant quantity of sulphur trioxide behind, which, if the process is continued long enough, crystallises from the residue when allowed to cool. In a similar manner it has been shown that sal-ammoniac when vaporised yields a mixture of ammonia and hydrogen chloride; that phosphoric chloride is split up into phosphorous chloride and chlorine; that ammonium carbonate is resolved into ammonia, water, and carbon dioxide. In all these and many other cases the dissociation proceeds gradually as the temperature is raised, till it becomes complete at a temperature which is peculiar to each case; it is promoted by reduction of pressure, and diminished by increase of pressure, or what is practically the same thing, by heating in an atmosphere consisting of one of the products of dissociation.

A history of the progress of thermo-chemistry, though professedly brief, would be in some danger of conveying an erroneous impression if a passing reference were not made to the nature of the work undertaken by other chemists and physicists who have occupied themselves with the subject. Among the rest, we owe to Marignac the determination of the specific heats of a number of saline solutions, and the thermal phenomena which ensue on diluting them (1870–76); to A. Horstmann a careful study of the progress of dissociation of a number of compounds, such as hydrogen iodide, ammonium chloride, ammonium carbonate (1868–78); to Alexander Naumann one of the earliest and most instructive systematic treatises on thermo-chemistry (*Grundriss der Thermochemie*, 1869); and lastly to Professor J. Willard Gibbs, the application of the principles of thermo-dynamics to many thermo-chemical problems.

CHAPTER II

THE CHEMICAL ELEMENTS: THEIR DISTRIBUTION IN NATURE, AND RECOGNITION BY THE CHEMIST

THE word "element," apart from poetical usage, is now universally understood to mean a substance which, though it may pass through many transformations, is always recoverable undiminished in quantity from any chemical combination into which it may enter, and is not by any known means resolvable into two or more distinct kinds of matter. Sulphur, for example, is regarded as an element, notwithstanding the allotropic changes which it undergoes under the influence of heat, because from sulphur in any of its known forms nothing can be abstracted which is not sulphur; in other words, it is homogeneous, and consists in its most minute parts of one kind of substance. On the other hand, water and iron rust are regarded as compounds because in proportion as, by suitable means, either of them is destroyed two kinds of new matter make their appearance, and the united weights of the products of "decomposition" are equal to the weight of the "compound" body from which they are educed. These ideas date from the time of Robert

Boyle. In his "Sceptical Chymist" (1680), he demonstrated the inconsistencies not only of the ancient Aristotelian doctrine of the Four Elements, but showed how little of foundation in fact and how much of imagination was to be found in the alchemical doctrine of the *Tria prima* current in his day.[1] Boyle not only insisted upon homogeneity as a characteristic of a true "element," but refused to admit any arguments but such as were based upon experiment.

The materials of which the earth and its inhabitants consist are chiefly compound, but they are resolvable into a limited number of substances, regarded for the present as elementary, because they have never yet been decompounded. Of these several—oxygen, nitrogen, and some other gases—are found in the atmosphere in the elemental form. The rest occur in proportions which are very unequal; some, as oxygen, silicon, carbon, and a few metals like aluminium, iron, calcium, magnesium, constituting in their various combinations the stuff out of which the greater part of the solid earth is formed, while others, though very necessary to the constitution of vegetable or animal tissue, occur in much smaller amount, and others again are found

---

[1] The complete title of Boyle's work sufficiently explains its object: "The Sceptical Chymist: or Chemico-physical Doubts and Paradoxes, touching the Experiments whereby vulgar Spagirists are wont to endeavour to evince their Salt, Sulphur, and Mercury to be the true Principles of Things, to which are subjoined divers Experiments and Notes about the *Producibleness of Chemical Principles.*"

only locally, or even in such minute quantity as to require special methods for their detection.

The recognition of new elementary substances does not necessarily imply, as often popularly supposed, the isolation of the element itself. Fluorspar, for example, was known in the middle of the last century to yield an acid analogous to muriatic acid (Scheele), but the element fluorine was not isolated till Moissan announced the results of his experiments in 1886. Similarly, alumina was known as a distinct earth in 1754 (Marggraff), but the metal was not obtained till 1828 (Wöhler). Potash, soda, lime, and magnesia were recognised and distinguished from one another long before their compound nature was even suspected, and so in many other cases. On the other hand, examples have been known of substances which, produced by methods calculated to afford the element, have been supposed to be simple, till long afterwards they have been found to be compound. This was the case with the metalloidal element titanium. A peculiar crystalline copper-coloured substance of metallic aspect, sometimes found in the bottom of blast-furnaces in which iron is reduced, was for a long time supposed to be metallic, that is elemental, titanium, till it was discovered by Wöhler to contain not only titanium, but carbon and nitrogen.

In 1837 fifty-four elements were known. In 1897 we recognise nearly eighty distinct substances believed to be elementary, notwithstanding that about ten of these have as yet been very imperfectly studied. From time to time new elements are announced, and while some of these "come like shadows" and "so depart," there is a tolerably steady addition of a permanently established member of the series on an average every three or four years. For these additions to our knowledge science is mainly indebted on the one hand to the introduction of previously unknown methods of experiment, and on the other hand to a closer attention to residual phenomena, previously neglected or imperfectly studied. As to the former, we need only refer to the application by Humphry Davy, in 1807, of the then recently discovered chemical effects of the electric current, by which he was led to the isolation of potassium and sodium; while the use of these metals in their turn afforded the means of decomposing compounds of boron, silicon, and aluminium with liberation of those elements.

In recent times the most fertile method of discovery of new elements has been the process called Spectrum Analysis. This was introduced as a definite method of experimental inquiry by Bunsen and Kirchhoff about 1859, and in Bunsen's hands led at once to the recognition of two previously unknown metals of the alkali group, to which he gave the names rubidium and cæsium. This discovery was followed by the isolation of thallium by Crookes in 1861, of indium by Reich and Richter in 1863, of gallium by De Boisbaudran in 1875 and of the oxide of an element called scandium by Nilson in 1879.

The story of Newton's experiments made in 1675 with the spectrum of the sun's rays is almost too familiar to require repetition. However, it is necessary to recall these experiments to mind in this place, because they not only form the basis upon which all subsequent discoveries with the prism were made, but they show what very important results often arise from apparently slight modifications in the mode of operating, or in the form of apparatus. Newton gives the following account of his procedure:[1] "In a very dark chamber, at a round hole about one-third part of an inch broad made in the shut of a window, I placed a glass prism, whereby the beam of the sun's light which came in at that hole might be refracted upwards towards the opposite wall of the chamber, and there form a coloured image of the sun. . . . This image was oblong and not oval, but terminated with two rectilinear and parallel sides and two semicircular ends. On its sides it was bounded pretty distinctly, but on its ends very confusedly and indistinctly, the light there decaying and vanishing by degrees. The breadth of this image answered to the sun's diameter, and was about two inches and the eighth part of an inch, including the penumbra. For the image was eighteen feet and a half distant from the prism; and at this distance that breadth, if

[1] Newton's "Opticks," Book i.

diminished by the diameter of the hole in window-shut, that is by a quarter of an inch, subtended an angle at the prism of about half a degree, which is the sun's apparent diameter. But the length of the image was about ten inches and a quarter, and the length of the rectilinear sides about eight inches, and the refracting angle of the prism whereby so great a length was made was 64°. With a less angle the length of the image was less, the breadth remaining the same. . . . Now, the different magnitude of the hole in the window-shut and different thickness of the prism where the rays passed through it, and different inclinations of the prism to the horizon, made no sensible changes in the length of the image. . . .

"This image or spectrum PT was coloured, being red at its least refracted end, T, and violet at its most refracted end, P, and yellow, green, and blue in the intermediate spaces, which agrees with the first proposition, that lights which differ in colour do also differ in refrangibility."

Newton further proved that "whiteness, and all grey colours between white and black, may be compounded of colours," and that "all homogeneal light has its proper colour answering to its degree of refrangibility, and that colour cannot be changed by reflections or refractions."

This represents the extent of knowledge regarding the nature of sunlight which remained for upwards of a century. What Newton saw in the spectrum upon the wall was a series of images of the sun so close together that they overlapped at their edges, forming a continuous band, having, as he says, parallel sides and circular ends. But the several rays which in sunlight are blended so as to give to the eye the sense of whiteness are separated in passing through the prism, so that the images overlapping give to the eye the impression of colour, those at the least refracted end being pure red, and those at the most refracted end being pure violet, while the intermediate spaces are filled by imperfectly separated rays of different degrees of refrangibility. If, however, a very narrow slit is used for the admission of the light, and a lens is interposed so as to throw a clear image of the slit upon the first face of the prism, which must be placed with its edges parallel to the slit, a new phenomenon may be observed when sunlight is used, and that is the appearance of fine black lines crossing the spectrum. These were first seen by Wollaston in 1802,[1] but were studied and mapped in 1814 by a German optician at Munich, Fraunhofer, and are generally known as Fraunhofer's lines. The physical cause of these black lines will be explained a little later; they are seen in the spectrum of sun-

---

[1] Wollaston (*Phil. Trans.* 1802) used for admission of the light a crevice $\frac{1}{20}$ inch broad. The beam was received by the eye close to the interposed prism, and four colours only were perceived, namely, red, yellowish green, blue, and violet. Wollaston seems to have regarded the few dark lines he saw as simply *boundaries* of these regions of colour.

light and of reflected sunlight, such as that which reaches us from the moon and the planets, but are not seen in the light derived from a heated solid, such as the lime in an oxyhydrogen lamp, or the carbon of an electric lamp. It has, however, long been known that flame may be coloured by putting into it various metals, salts, and other vaporisable substances, and the light thus obtained, when seen through a prism, gives separate bright lines standing in the order of their refrangibilities, but separated by dark spaces. Some of these were described by Sir John Herschel in 1822, and again by Professor W. A. Miller in 1845. It was not until 1859, however, that the position and colour of the lines seen in the spectra of metallic salts vaporised in a flame were employed systematically for the recognition of such substances, and the foundation of the spectroscopic method of analysis was laid by Bunsen and Kirchhoff. The apparatus employed is in principle very simple. The light to be examined passes through a narrow slit, the edges of which are parallel with the edges of the prism. To concentrate the light after entering the slit, it passes through a tube containing a pair of lenses by which the rays are made parallel before entering the prism. On leaving the prism the spectrum is seen through a telescope, which gives a magnified image of it. The arrangement commonly adopted is shown in the figures which are to be found in nearly all text-books of physics.

Now, when the flame of a Bunsen lamp is placed before the slit, and a platinum wire dipped into a solution of, say, common salt, is introduced into the flame, a bright yellow light is seen, and looking into the telescope a bright yellow line is seen, and nothing else.[1] If for a sodium compound we substitute a salt of potassium, then a red line is seen near the less refrangible end; if a lithium compound, a red line is seen nearer to the yellow than the red potassium line, and also a yellow line, which is not far from the sodium line, but not coincident with it. In like manner other metals give colorations to flame, or their compounds give colorations, which in the spectroscope are resolved into bright lines separated usually by dark spaces, each line having an invariable position relatively to the others.

The method of spectrum analysis is distinguished by its extraordinary delicacy from the ordinary chemical methods, which are chiefly based upon the production of colours or precipitates in liquids. Bunsen and Kirchhoff in their Memoir[2] show that, for example, in the case of sodium the eye can recognise the presence of one three-millionth of a milligramme of the metal. Hence the common production of the yellow light in the Bunsen flame, when a platinum wire, apparently clean, is held in it, or when the air is but slightly agitated, so as to

[1] This really consists of two yellow lines so close together that the simple spectroscope is usually incompetent to show them separate.

[2] Translated into several English journals; *e.g. Phil. Mag.*, vol. xx. (1860), and *Jour. Chem. Soc.*, xiii. (1861), 270.

raise a little common dust. Sodium, in the form chiefly of common salt, is to be found in minute quantity distributed in the atmosphere everywhere; it is present in all common water, and in nearly all animal and vegetable substances, and the frequent appearance of the yellow light, and the corresponding yellow double line, was a source of much perplexity to the earlier observers, who, finding nothing else to account for it, attributed it not unnaturally to the presence of water. It was not till 1856 that Professor Swan of St. Andrews recognised in sodium the cause of the yellow line.

Thus far reference has been made only to the effect of introducing into a flame substances which are capable of being converted into vapour by the heat, and so carried up in that state into the upper part of the flame, where the vapour becomes incandescent and gives out light. In some cases, however, the temperature of a common flame is not sufficiently high to give this effect. For example, many metals are not vaporised by such a source of heat, and it is necessary to resort to the much hotter electric "arc," or to the electric spark obtained from an induction coil, in order to produce vapour from them, and cause this vapour to emit light. The induction coil is specially serviceable in such cases, for sparks may be taken between the poles tipped with the metal under examination, or may be made to pass between one pole and a solution of the substance to be tested without any appreciable loss of material. It must, however, be remembered that the spectra observed under these circumstances are not identical with those which would be obtained from the same element at the lower temperature of a flame; the spectrum afforded by a given elementary substance in the arc or spark is in almost all cases more complex, that is, it exhibits a greater number of lines than when a flame is used. The spectrum observable when a flame is coloured by the introduction of a salt is, in many cases, made up of comparatively broad bands, and these disappear when the temperature is raised, being replaced by bright narrower lines in different positions, not coincident with those of the bands. These lines usually remain unchanged at still more elevated temperatures, but other additional lines frequently make their appearance. The spectrum derived from the flame is, in such cases, usually attributed to the glowing vapour of a compound, while the line spectrum obtained by the use of the arc or the spark is supposed to be that of the metal present. These are quite distinct from each other, and at present there is no recognisable relation of the spectrum of a metallic element to that of its compounds, such as the oxide or chloride.

As to the non-metallic elements, and especially the gases hydrogen, oxygen, nitrogen, the light which they give out at high temperatures is less intense than that emitted by metallic vapours; and they are usually observed most conveniently by allowing an electric discharge to pass through the gas confined in a glass tube, and expanded by means of an air-pump till the pressure of the gas is reduced to something very small. The discharge under such conditions passes through a much longer column of the gas, which becomes incandescent throughout. As with the metals, the character of the spectrum varies according to conditions: at comparatively low temperatures bands of light or closely grouped lines are seen; at higher temperatures these change in position, ultimately disappearing as the temperature is raised, and giving place to separate fine lines, the relative intensities of which, however, change with altered conditions in a manner which is often very difficult to explain. It seems established that the number and positions of the lines forming a given spectrum are dependent partly upon the composition or molecular constitution of the substance employed, partly upon the quantity or density of its vapour, and partly upon the temperature to which it is exposed.

These variations, however, perplexing as they are to the inexperienced observer, do not prevent the application of the spectroscope to the recognition of a great many elements, and, as already stated, have led to the discovery of several. The presence of several elements together does not interfere under ordinary circumstances with the exhibition by each of its own special array of lines, and hence complex mixtures, of minerals for example, may be submitted to examination by the spectroscope, with the certainty that those constituents which are capable of yielding vapour will be recognisable, notwithstanding that they are present in only minute quantity. Naturally, however, when heat is applied, the more volatile constituents will pass off in vapour first, and will therefore afford their spectra more readily than the less volatile.

Reference has already been made to the fact that sunlight differs from the light emitted by heated solid bodies, inasmuch as the band of colour is not continuous from end to end, but exhibits a large number of fine black lines crossing it transversely, which are known as Fraunhofer's lines. Notwithstanding that Fraunhofer counted and mapped some hundreds of these lines, he did not give any explanation of their occurrence, and it was only many years later that the solution of the mystery was supplied by Kirchhoff. When a vapour is heated strongly enough it gives out light which consists of rays possessing definite refrangibility, and capable of exciting the sensation of colour in the eye, as already stated; at lower temperatures, however, the vapour is capable of stopping the same radiations. Hence, if a sufficiently thick layer of such vapour is interposed in the path of a ray of light from a source which supplies a continuous spectrum, a series of black lines would appear in the same position as the bright lines which would be seen if the vapour itself gave out light and this was viewed through a prism. The sun is supposed to be a very hot, solid, or fluid body, the light from which, if uninterrupted, would afford a continuous spectrum, like that given by a heated solid metal, or by heated lime. But this luminescent nucleus is surrounded by an atmosphere of vapours less hot, and therefore capable of stopping certain of the radiations; and so black lines appear in the spectrum of the sun's light, and these correspond in position to the bright lines given by such metals as iron, calcium, sodium, and other terrestrial elements when their vapours are heated to incandescence. Similar observations have led to the belief that a large number of elements are common to the earth, and to the sun, and many of the stars.

With regard to the recognition of elemental bodies, however, a distinction must be drawn between the recognition of wholly unknown and unsuspected new substances, and the discovery of methods for isolating from known compounds elements the existence of which is already well established. As already stated, potash and soda were distinguished from each other many years before their compound nature was demonstrated, and potassium and sodium obtained in the metallic state; alumina and silica were familiar long before the elements aluminium and silicon were separated from their associated oxygen. One of the most interesting cases of this kind is afforded by the non-metallic element fluorine. Fluoride of calcium is widely diffused in nature. It occurs in many minerals, and, in small quantity, as a constituent of the tissues of plants and animals. It is well known in the crystalline form as the beautiful fluor or Derbyshire spar. The action of sulphuric acid upon this substance was studied by Scheele in the middle of the last century, and the acid so produced, long employed for etching glass, has been recognised since the time of Davy as a compound of the same nature as muriatic acid; that is to say, as constituted of hydrogen associated with an element having properties similar to those of chlorine. Nevertheless the separation of this element, long called fluorine, from the compounds in which it is known to reside has only been accomplished after a long series of fruitless attempts. Fluorine in the so-called free state is the most energetic chemical agent known. It decomposes water in consequence of its affinity for hydrogen, and the displaced oxygen is partly converted into ozone. It combines with metals of all kinds, and the heat generated by its union with silicon, with sulphur, with iodine, and even with carbon is so great as to cause ignition of those substances. It is not displaced from its compounds by the action of any other known element, and the statements concerning its liberation from mercuric or silver fluorides by the action of chlorine were erroneously based upon imperfect experiments. It is obtainable, though with difficulty, by heating certain fluorides, notably ceric fluoride, CeF_4, and plumbic fluoride, PbF_4 (Brauner), which thus become reduced to lower fluorides. But the knowledge of this remarkable substance would have remained extremely imperfect but for Moissan's experiments in 1886 on the electrolysis of anhydrous hydrogen fluoride. This liquid is not an electrolyte, but on the addition of dry potassium hydrogen fluoride it conducts, and the salt is resolved into fluorine and potassium. The latter liberates hydrogen which escapes from the surface of the cathode, while the former is set free at the anode in the form of a pale greenish gas which possesses all the chemical activity of chlorine in an exalted degree. It is liquefiable at about $-190°$, and its boiling point under atmospheric pressure is very close to $-187°$ C. It forms at this temperature a pale yellow liquid, which no longer exhibits the energetic chemical properties displayed by the gas, for at this low temperature it does not even displace iodine from iodides, though it retains the power of seizing the hydrogen in benzene or oil of turpentine with incandescence. The powerful affinity of fluorine for hydrogen is the last to disappear.

We may now turn by way of contrast to the discovery in the atmosphere of a new gas, or rather a mixture of gases, the existence of which there had been no reason for suspecting, and the strange characters of which could never have been predicted from any consideration within the range of recognised chemical philosophy. The history of the discovery of "argon" is one of the most interesting and instructive chapters in the records of natural science. For some time previously to 1893 Lord Rayleigh had been making determinations of the densities of the principal gases,[1] nitrogen among the rest, and his attention was early attracted to a curious anomaly observed in the case of this element. When the gas was made from ammonia it was found to be decidedly lighter than when obtained from air, and as it seemed "certain that the abnormal lightness cannot be explained by contamination with hydrogen, or with ammonia, or with water," everything seemed to suggest "that the explanation is to be sought in a dissociated state of the nitrogen itself." And by successive experiments it was shown that whether the oxygen of air was removed by red-hot copper, by red-hot iron, or by cold ferrous hydrate, the superior density of atmospheric nitrogen remained undiminished, while the density of nitrogen obtained by various chemical processes from nitrous oxide and from nitric oxide was the same as that from ammonia. The mean weights of nitrogen held by a certain globe were as follows:—

From nitric oxide	2·3001	
From nitrous oxide	2·2990	Mean 2·2993
From ammonium nitrite	2·2987	
From air by hot copper	2·3103	Mean 2·3102
From air by hot iron	2·3100	Difference ·0109
From air by ferrous hydrate	2·3102	

[1] *Proc. R. S.*, liii. 134.

Hence, after due corrections, one litre of chemical nitrogen weighs 1·2505 gram; atmospheric nitrogen weighs 1·2572 gram. A review of all these facts led to the conclusion that the lightness of chemical nitrogen was not to be attributed to the presence of any familiar impurity, or to the existence of two forms of nitrogen, but rather that the greater density of atmospheric nitrogen was due to its association with a heavier gas existing in the air in small quantity, and hitherto unrecognised. The question as to the homogeneousness of the gaseous residue left when the oxygen of air, the moisture, and the carbon dioxide have all been withdrawn, was long ago considered by Cavendish in his "Experiments on Air," published in the *Philosophical Transactions* for 1785. Here he says, "As far as the experiments hitherto published extend, we scarcely know more of the nature of the phlogisticated [1] part of our atmosphere, than that it is not diminished by lime-water, caustic alkalis, or nitrous air; that it is unfit to support fire or maintain life in animals; and that its specific gravity is not much less than that of common air; so that though the nitrous acid, by being united to phlogiston,[2] is converted into air possessed of these properties, and, consequently, though it was reasonable to suppose that part at least of the phlogisticated air of the atmosphere

---

[1] Phlogisticated air is the term, in the language of the theory of phlogiston, for nitrogen; dephlogisticated air is oxygen.

[2] *i.e.* deprived of oxygen.

consists of this acid united to phlogiston, yet it might fairly be doubted whether the whole is of this kind, or whether there are not in reality many different substances compounded together by us under the name of phlogisticated air. I therefore made an experiment to determine whether the whole of a given portion of the phlogisticated air of the atmosphere could be reduced to nitrous acid, or whether there was not a part of a different nature from the rest which would refuse to undergo that change." Cavendish then proceeds to describe his experiment, from which he concludes that "if there is any part of the phlogisticated air of our atmosphere which differs from the rest, and cannot be reduced to nitrous acid, we may safely conclude that it is not more than $\frac{1}{120}$ part of the whole." There the question was left more than a century ago. In August 1894 it was answered by the announcement by Lord Rayleigh and Professor Ramsay of the discovery of a new constituent of the atmosphere, a gas having a density nearly half as large again as that of nitrogen, and distinguished from all then known gases by absolute chemical inertness, being, so far as at present known, incapable of entering into any form of chemical combination.

Two methods have been employed by the discoverers for the removal of the nitrogen and the isolation of the argon. The first was the method used by Cavendish, though with the advantage of modern appliances. This consists in adding oxygen to the air confined over a solution of caustic potash, and then passing electric sparks through the gaseous mixture. The nitrogen is thus made to unite with oxygen, and the resulting oxide of nitrogen is absorbed by the potash, and is converted into nitrite and nitrate. At the end of the experiment the residual oxygen is easily removable by red-hot copper or otherwise. The other process consists in first absorbing the oxygen from the air operated on by means of red-hot copper, and then getting rid of the nitrogen by passing the gas over the surface of magnesium, or better still, a mixture of lime and metallic magnesium. Either of these agents absorbs nitrogen, forming solid magnesium or calcium nitride, leaving the argon as a colourless gas.

The discovery of argon among the atmospheric gases naturally led to a search for a more productive source of the element, and the attention of Professor Ramsay was drawn to the statement that certain minerals containing uranium evolve under the action of dilute sulphuric acid a gas which was supposed to be nitrogen. On submitting some of the gas thus obtained to the process of sparking in admixture with oxygen very little contraction occurred, and it was manifest that the amount of nitrogen present was insignificant. On examination of the light afforded by the expanded gas exposed to the spark discharge, it showed at once a feature which gave a clue to the character of the new substance. In addition to lines due to hydrogen and argon, present in the gas, a brilliant yellow line was observed, nearly, but not quite coincident with the yellow line D_1 of sodium. The wave-length of this line is 587·49 millionths of a millimetre, and it is exactly coincident with the line D_3 in the solar chromosphere attributed to the solar element, which has been named by Lockyer *helium*. The complete spectrum is characterised by five very brilliant lines in the red, yellow, blue-green, blue, and violet respectively. The gas is chemically inert like argon, and, like that element, in molecular constitution it appears to be monatomic. The difficulty of complete separation from argon renders the determinations which have been made of its density somewhat uncertain, but helium is undoubtedly, next to hydrogen, the lightest gas known, and its specific gravity has been observed as somewhat less than 2. Whether it will be further reduced is a matter for future experiment.

This remarkable history, however, does not end here, for early in June 1898 Professor Ramsay and Mr. M. W. Travers communicated to the Royal Society an account of their examination of liquid air, in which they announced the discovery of a new constituent, to which they have given the name *krypton* (hidden). Ten days later, in a further paper, they described two other gases, named respectively *neon* (new) and *metargon*, among the " Companions of Argon." The method employed consisted in liquefying a large amount—nearly 18 litres—of "argon," obtained from atmospheric air by absorbing the oxygen by red-hot copper, and the nitrogen by magnesium. The argon in the liquid state was accompanied by a considerable quantity of a solid substance. When the temperature was allowed to rise, the liquid evaporated away, the first portions of gas being collected separately, as likely to contain any substance lighter than argon. The old argon then boiled off, and was collected in a gas-holder, while the solid, of which mention has been made, evaporated last, and was collected by itself. The lightest and most volatile ingredient of this mixture, called neon, is a gas whose density is believed to be about 11, while argon has a density approaching 20. The solid matter gave a gas having a density nearly identical with that of argon, and since it has been found to be, like argon, both monatomic and chemically inert, though exhibiting a different spectrum, it has been named metargon. The gases thus isolated from air seem to agree in the common characteristic of chemical inactivity, or inability to form compounds. They are believed to be monatomic, that is, that, like mercury vapour, their molecules contain one atom only; but as their densities have only been estimated very roughly, in consequence of the difficulty of separating them completely from one another, the atomic weights of the most recently discovered are still very doubtful. The values assigned to them provisionally are as follows:—

Name.	Symbol.	Atomic or Molecular Weight.
Helium	He	4
Neon	Ne	22
Argon	A	40
Metargon	Aμ	40
Krypton	Kr	80

Quite recently small quantities of hydrogen are said to have been detected in atmospheric air by M. Gautier, so that our atmosphere is a mixture even more complex than had ever been previously suspected. The new gases are probably physiologically as well as chemically inert; but whether there may not be still lurking, undetected in the vast ocean of gas at the bottom of which all human affairs are transacted, some small quantity of hitherto unrecognised but physiologically active ingredients, is a question to which for the present there is no answer.

CHAPTER III

RECTIFICATION AND STANDARDISATION OF ATOMIC WEIGHTS

THE necessity for preserving the distinction between *fact* established by observation or experiment, and *hypothesis* which suggests an explanation of the facts, has not always been clearly recognised in chemistry. We know, for example, that oxygen and hydrogen will combine together in certain proportions, and in no others. This is explained by the *assumption* that atoms of oxygen unite with atoms of hydrogen to form compounds, and that the atoms of oxygen are all of equal mass, and are each nearly sixteen times heavier than an atom of hydrogen. It is therefore impossible that there can be compounds made up of complex proportions of these two elements, unless we assume that which is very improbable, namely, that the atoms combine in large numbers and uneven proportions, say, for example, thirty of one kind to thirty-one of the other. Dalton was the first to apply the "atomic theory" to chemistry, and his ideas respecting chemical combination were expressed somewhat in the following manner:[1] "When two elements

[1] Thomson's "System of Chemistry," 3rd edition, vol. iii. 1807.

combine to form a third substance, it is to be presumed that *one* atom of one joins to *one* atom of the other, unless when some reason can be assigned for supposing the contrary. Thus oxygen and hydrogen unite together and form water. We are to presume that an atom of water is formed by the combination of *one* atom of oxygen with *one* atom of hydrogen. In like manner *one* atom of ammonia is formed by the combination of *one* atom of azote with *one* atom of hydrogen." It is obvious that if such hypothetical ideas are superimposed upon the acknowledged facts as to the composition of water, an artificial rule is established for estimating the relative atomic weights; and in Dalton's time, and chiefly as the outcome of his experiments, the values attributed to the atomic weights of the three elements referred to above were actually based on this combination of ideas. Dalton, however, and all his successors, were obliged to admit that this simple hypothesis is not applicable to all cases, and is manifestly often opposed to well-established facts. The composition of water, for example, was represented by nearly all chemists during the former half of this century by the formula HO, in which H stands for 1 part by weight of hydrogen, and O for 8 parts by weight of oxygen. The change which has resulted in the universal adoption of the formula H_2O, in which O is approximately twice 8, was the result of a protracted controversy beginning from the time of Dalton himself. Gay-Lussac's celebrated "Memoir on the combination of Gaseous Substances with each other,"[1] was published in 1809, and the Essay[1] by Avogadro, on "A Manner of determining the relative Masses of the Elementary Molecules of Bodies, and the Proportions in which they enter into these Compounds," in 1811. But while Gay-Lussac's facts have always been admitted, except for a time by Dalton, the hypothesis of Avogadro has been generally adopted only within the last thirty years.

The nature of the problem will be shown most clearly if we consider closely a single example, that of oxygen. Nearly eight parts of oxygen unite with one part of hydrogen to form water, but the question is, whether in the smallest existing particle, that is the molecule, of water there is but one atom of oxygen with one atom of hydrogen, as Dalton supposed, or whether water may not contain more than one atom of either or both these elements; and whether, taking the atomic weight of hydrogen as the unit, that of oxygen should be 8 or some multiple of 8 ? The question began to be seriously discussed when, in 1843, Gerhardt proposed to use the hypothesis of Avogadro as the basis for a common measure of molecules. If it be true, as Avogadro taught, that "equal volumes of different gases at the same temperature and pressure contain the same number of molecules," then those quantities of all substances which fill the same volume in

---

[1] English translations of both are included in No. 4 of the "Alembic Club Reprints."

the state of gas must be taken as molecular proportions under the same conditions.

Previously to this time there had been no rule commonly recognised and applied to this purpose. Thus, if the symbol H stand for one volume of hydrogen gas, HO (O = 8) represents also one volume of water vapour, and HCl represents two volumes of hydrogen chloride gas. Or if HO stand for two volumes, then H must also stand for two volumes, and HCl for four volumes. Gerhardt proposed to take water as the standard of comparison; that is, as the unit of molecular magnitude. He represented the molecule of water by the formula H_2O (H = 1 and O = 16), reviving the relative value of the atomic weight attributed to oxygen by Berzelius, though now reduced to the scale in which H is taken as 1, instead of O as 100. Accordingly the formulæ H_2O, HCl, NH_3, CO_2 represent equal volumes of the several compounds in the gaseous state, and under the same conditions of temperature and pressure. And it is necessary to observe that these formulæ do not only agree in regard to the hypothetical, physical constitution of the gases which they represent; that is, they comply with the hypothesis of Avogadro, but they actually represent the chemically reactive units or molecules of these substances. But these formulæ imply that the atomic weights of oxygen and carbon must be assumed to be double of those commonly adopted by chemistry at the time, and require a corresponding change in the formulæ of all the oxides, acids, bases, and other compounds in which these elements exist. Great support for these views was derived from the successive discoveries of the constitution of ether by Williamson (1850), and of many acid anhydrides by Gerhardt himself.[1] For so long as ether was regarded as the oxide of ethyl, C_4H_5O, while alcohol represented a compound of this oxide with water, namely, as hydrated oxide of ethyl, $C_4H_5O + HO$ ($C = 6$, $O = 8$), the relation was not perceptible. But when Williamson showed that the conversion of alcohol into ether is accomplished, not by the simple withdrawal of water from alcohol, but as a consequence of the exchange of an atom of hydrogen in alcohol for another ethyl group, C_4H_5, the resulting compound forming a volume of vapour equal to the standard volume, namely, to the volume occupied by a molecular proportion of water, H_2O, a new view of the constitution of alcohol followed as a necessary consequence. The following comparison will show clearly the nature of the change involved :—

OLD STYLE.		NEW STYLE.	
Formula: [$O=8$, $C=6$]	Corresponding Volume of Vapour.	Formula: [$O=16$, $C=12$]	Corresponding Volume of Vapour.
HO	1 vol.	H_2O	2 vols.
HCl	2 vols.	HCl	2 ,,
CO	1 vol.	CO	2 ,,
CO_2	1 vol.	CO_2	2 ,,
NH_3	2 vols.	NH_3	2 ,,
C_4H_5O	1 vol.	$C_4H_{10}O$	2 ,,
$C_4H_5O + HO$	2 vols.	C_2H_6O	2 ,,

---

[1] See further on, Chap. V.

It was, however, long before such views as these received the general assent of the chemical world, and it required the support of evidence drawn from various apparently distinct lines of inquiry, to establish firmly the new doctrine. In order to ascertain the volume of vapour which corresponds to a given formula, it is only necessary to determine the specific gravity of the vapour, that is, the weight of one unit volume, hydrogen or air being usually taken as the standard. But though text-books of this period usually gave an account of the methods of Dumas and Gay-Lussac for such experimental determinations, the results were treated as isolated physical facts, and were seldom or never applied to the correction of formulæ, and their reduction to a common standard.

In 1834 Dumas discovered the remarkable fact that chlorine is capable of replacing an equal volume of hydrogen in many organic compounds, the process being afterwards known as substitution, or, as Dumas called it, *metalepsy*. Acetic acid, for example, is a monobasic acid, for it affords with each metal, as a rule, only one salt, in the formation of which one equivalent of the acid was known to interact with one equivalent of such a base as potash. But three-fourths of the hydrogen of acetic acid is exchangeable in three successive stages for equivalent quantities of chlorine, giving rise to mono-, di-, and trichloracetic acids, thus:—

Acetic acid	$C_4H_3O_3HO$ ($C=6$, $O=8$)
Monochloracetic acid	$C_4H_2ClO_3HO$
Dichloracetic acid	$C_4HCl_2O_3HO$
Trichloracetic acid	$C_4Cl_3O_3HO$

These chlorinated acids are monobasic, and bear a strong resemblance to acetic acid, from which they are derived.[1]

Dumas also pointed out,[2] in reply to criticisms from Berzelius, that while chloracetic acid heated with potash splits into carbon dioxide and chloroform, acetic acid heated with baryta gives carbon dioxide and a gas which he identified with marsh gas, of which chloroform is the trichloro-derivative, and therefore an analogue. And taking the principle of isomorphism as a guide, he declared that compounds like acetic acid and chloracetic acid belong to the same *chemical type*, just as all the different varieties of alum belong to the same crystallographic or mechanical type. A little later he studied the action of chlorine upon marsh gas, and though he did not succeed in isolating all the successive products of the substitute of chlorine for hydrogen in this compound, he obtained and analysed the perchloride, which is the final product of the action, and showed that the production of this compound and chloroform represented two stages in the same process. The complete series of substitution products would be expressed by the following names and formulæ:—

Methane or marsh gas	CHHHH.
Chloromethane or methyl chloride	CHHHCl.
Dichloromethane or methylene dichloride	CHHClCl.
Trichloromethane or chloroform	CHClClCl.
Tetrachloromethane or carbon tetrachloride	CClClClCl.

---

[1] *Compt. Rend.*, vii. 474 (1838).
[2] *Annalen d. Chem. u. Pharm.*, xxxiii. 179, 259 (1840).

These successive steps have since that time been completely traced, and each of these compounds is now well known and characterised. Dumas also, together with Stas, investigated the action of potash upon a number of alcohols and their principal ethers, and showed[1] that all true alcohols can produce a corresponding acid. Thus he was led to a classification of carbon compounds according to the nature of the typical substance, alcohol, ether, acetic acid, aldehyd, &c., from which the compound could be derived, actually or hypothetically, by a process of substitution.

As will be shown in a later chapter, the molecules of water, ammonia, hydrochloric acid, hydrogen, and marsh gas were afterwards successively adopted as types of the various classes of chemical compounds, and thus a classification was effected of the otherwise miscellaneous products of successive discoveries, especially in the domain of what has so long been called "organic" chemistry. Though it was many years before this doctrine was generally accepted, the important fact came ultimately to be recognised that certain elements are distinguished by the power of holding together two or more atoms of other elements, or of "residues" consisting of several elements united into a group.[2]

In water, for example, and in all the immediate

---

[1] *Ann. Chim. Phys.* [2], lxxiii. 73 (1840).
[2] A fuller account of these developments is reserved for a later chapter (Chap. V.).

derivatives of water, such as caustic potash, alcohol, ether, silver oxide, hypochlorous acid, it was perceived that while the electro-positive elements, such as hydrogen, potassium, ethyl, &c., could be separately replaced, and that in water the hydrogen is divisible into two exactly equal parts, the oxygen maintains its *indivisibility* throughout. This important distinction is recorded in the formulæ of the water type:—

$$\left.\begin{matrix}H\\H\end{matrix}\right\}O \quad \left.\begin{matrix}K\\H\end{matrix}\right\}O \quad \left.\begin{matrix}K\\K\end{matrix}\right\}O \quad \left.\begin{matrix}C_2H\\H\end{matrix}\right\}O.$$

$$\left.\begin{matrix}C_2H_5\\C_2H_5\end{matrix}\right\}O \quad \left.\begin{matrix}Ag\\Ag\end{matrix}\right\}O \quad \left.\begin{matrix}H\\Cl\end{matrix}\right\}O.$$

Gerhardt pointed out that the formula H_2O for water is preferable to the formula HO ($O = 8$) then in use, because it is consistent with the fact that each monatomic (in modern language, monad or univalent) radicle gives two derivatives of the water type, that is, by successive replacement of the two atoms of hydrogen it forms two oxides,[1] like caustic potash and oxide of potassium, as shown by the above formulæ. The same radicle, however, gives only one chloride, one bromide, and one iodide.

Precisely similar considerations can be applied to compounds containing carbon. Marsh gas is composed of this element united with hydrogen, but whereas the latter can be replaced by chlorine, or other agents, in four separate and equal portions, the carbon is not only not so divisible, but it has

[1] *Traité de Chimie Organique*, t. iv. 589.

the power of linking together in one definite and homogeneous compound the chlorine which has been introduced in exchange for a part of the hydrogen, and the residue of hydrogen which is left after such operation. Hence such compounds as CH_3Cl and $CHCl_3$ are producible from marsh gas, and are by an inverse operation transformable back again into that compound. These relations are sufficiently indicated by the formulæ already given (p. 66).

Further, if we examine the now familiar series of homologous hydrocarbons, alcohols, aldehyds, acids, &c., containing carbon in progressively increasing proportion, it becomes obvious that each term of such series differs from the next below and the next above by a quantity of carbon which is never less than 12 parts by weight, the quantity of oxygen, if present, remaining the same throughout the series. The following formulæ, for example, represent all the known members of the several series of paraffins, alcohols, and fatty acids:—

Paraffins.	Alcohols.	Fatty Acids.
C_xH_4	C_xH_4O	$C_xH_2O_2$
$C_{2x}H_6$	$C_{2x}H_6O$	$C_{2x}H_4O_2$
$C_{3x}H_8$	$C_{3x}H_8O$	$C_{3x}H_6O_2$
$C_{4x}H_{10}$	$C_{4x}H_{10}O$	$C_{4x}H_8O_2$
$C_{5x}H_{12}$	$C_{5x}H_{12}O$	$C_{5x}H_{10}O_2$
&c.	&c.	&c.

It is obvious that in such series x must be equal to 1, and the atomic weight of carbon must be 12, and not a smaller number such as 6. For supposing $C = 6$, then each formula would represent the proportion of carbon present as divisible into two equal parts, for which there is no justification in fact. Moreover, in such a series as the paraffins, there would be on that hypothesis a gas composed of carbon and hydrogen having half the density of marsh gas, and the formula CH_2. It is almost needless to say that such a gas is not known. A similar argument may be based upon the well-established fact that in the numerous definite decompositions in which the oxides of carbon are evolved, none are known in which carbon is eliminated in this form in quantity less than would be expressed by 12 parts by weight. Take formic acid, for example—

$$C_xH_2O_2 - H_2O = C_xO$$
$$C_xH_2O_2 + O = C_xO_2 + H_2O$$

If $C = 6$ these quantities would have to be represented as C_2O and C_2O_2 respectively, which would be unnecessary and illogical, so long as C_2 is known to represent an indivisible quantity.

Throughout this long discussion, extending over twenty years or more, two chief considerations were gradually brought to one common focus; the one based upon the hypothesis of Avogadro provides a uniform measure of molecular magnitudes, the other indicates the limited combining capacity of each elementary atom, and of each group of atoms forming a radicle. If to this is superadded the strictly chemical process which consists in ascertaining by experiment whether the quantity of any given element, found in a series of molecules of which it is a common ingredient, is divisible into several equal parts, or is not so divisible, we arrive at the conclusion that the indivisible or atomic proportions of each element can be determined. And the end of it is, that taking one part by weight of hydrogen as the unit for the scale of atomic weights, and finding that not less than 16 such parts by weight of oxygen ever enter into or leave a molecule of a compound, 16 must be regarded as the atomic weight of this element. By a similar course of reasoning applied to the compounds of carbon, silicon, sulphur and its allies, it is now agreed that the value assigned to the atomic weights of each of these elements must be, as in the case of oxygen, double the value previously assumed, so that henceforth C stands for 12 parts of carbon, S for 32 parts of sulphur, and so forth.

The new atomic weights and the simultaneous changes in the system of chemical formulæ were, however, not generally adopted in text-books or in scientific memoirs till long after 1860. The new system was employed for the first time by Hofmann in his lectures at the Royal College of Chemistry in the year 1861, and this example doubtless assisted greatly to promote the recognition of the new doctrine in England. In 1864 Dr. Odling, as President of the Chemical Section of the British Association, was able to congratulate the section upon "the substantial agreement which now prevails among

English chemists as to the combining proportions of the elementary bodies and the molecular weights of their most important compounds." But in France the formula for water continued very generally to be written HO, or occasionally, with equal impropriety, H_2O_2, down to a period at least five-and-twenty years later. So great, even in science, is the influence of habit and of authority in retarding the modification of long settled ideas.

The application of the "law" of Avogadro to the settlement of atomic weights is, however, limited by the fact that certain elements, metals, appear to be incapable of producing compounds which are vaporisable without decomposition. Thus silver, gold, platinum, copper, and cobalt form no volatile chloride or other compound of which the vapour density could be ascertained. In such cases recourse must be had to other methods, whereof the most important is the application of the specific heat, in accordance with the discovery of Petit and Dulong published in 1819. These physicists found that when the number expressing the specific heat of a solid element is multiplied by the atomic weight of the same, the numerical value of the product is nearly constant. This is shown in the following table:—

COPY OF TABLE BY PETIT AND DULONG.[1]

	Specific Heats.	Atomic Weights (O=1).	Atomic Weight ×Specific Heat.
Bismuth	·0288	13·30	·3830
Lead	·0293	12·95	·3794
Gold	·0298	12·43	·3704
Platinum	·0314	11·16	·3740
Tin	·0514	7·35	·3779
Silver	·0557	6·75	·3759
Zinc	·0927	4·03	·3736
Tellurium	·0912	4·03	·3675
Copper	·0949	3·957	·3755
Nickel	·1035	3·69	·3819
Iron	·1100	3·392	·3731
Cobalt	·1498	2·46	·3685
Sulphur	·1880	2·011	·3780

The statement of the relation indicated in the last column of figures is expressed in the following words of the authors, p. 405: "Les atomes de tous les corps simples ont exactement la même capacité pour la chaleur."

Of course several of the values inserted in this table have since been proved to be exceedingly inaccurate, but more modern researches have established the general truth of the principle here enunciated. The system of atomic weights at present in use is referred to hydrogen as unity, but the scale upon which the atomic weight is calculated makes no difference except in the absolute value of the product, approximately constant, obtained by multiplying together the specific heat and the atomic weight.

[1] *Ann. Chim. Phys.*, 1819, x. 403.

On the hydrogen scale this product is about 6·4, and the process of settling an atomic weight is very simply based on the equation—

$$\text{Atomic Wt.} \times \text{Spec. Heat} = 6\cdot 4,$$

from which, if the specific heat is known, the atomic weight can be at once roughly calculated. Since, however, the experimental difficulties attending the determination of the specific heat are greater than those which are involved in the determination of the combining proportion of an element, the numbers expressing specific heats are less exact than those which express combining weight. The atomic weight is either identical with the combining proportion, or is some multiple of it. So that, in order to fix the atomic weight of a metal, we take that multiple of the equivalent or combining proportion which comes nearest to the value of this product. The specific heat of tin, for example, is ·0559 (Bunsen), and 29·75 parts of the metal combine with an equivalent of chlorine. Then, since At. Wt. $= \dfrac{6\cdot 4}{\text{Spec. H}} = \dfrac{6\cdot 4}{.0559} = 114\cdot 5$, the atomic weight is taken to be $29\cdot 75 \times 4$, or 119·0, or thereabouts, rather than 29·75 or any smaller multiple of this number.

It is interesting and important to note that whenever the two methods, based on the use of the law of Avogadro on the one hand and that of Petit and Dulong on the other, can be applied to the same element the results agree. Thus nickel is known to have an atomic weight which approaches 59, for the specific heat is ·108 and $\frac{6\cdot 4}{\cdot 108} = 59\cdot 2$. Also the vapour density of its carbonyl compound is 86·5 compared with hydrogen. Hence the molecular weight of this compound is 173, and it is found by analysis to contain 33·3 per cent. of nickel; 173 parts therefore contain 57·6 parts of nickel, which is in practical agreement with the value derived from the specific heat. But just as the law of Avogadro had to wait nearly fifty years for general recognition, so the principle asserted by Petit and Dulong remained unapplied and almost unnoticed, save casually as a matter of curiosity, down to the present generation. It is true that Regnault, as a result of his researches, commenced in 1840,[1] was led to regard the law as universally applicable, but Kopp, who resumed the question a quarter of a century later, came to the conclusion[2] that the law of Dulong and Petit is not strictly valid, even when the exceptional cases of boron, carbon, and silicon are excluded. The want of *exact* concordance among the products of the multiplication of specific heat by atomic weight does not, however, prevent the very general application of the law for the purpose of controlling atomic weights in the manner already described. And chemistry is indebted chiefly to the representations of Cannizzaro[3] in 1858 for the recognition of this most important use of the observed relations.

[1] Especially *Ann. Ch. Phys.* [2], lxxiii. 66, and [3] xxvi. 261, and xlvi. 257.
[2] *Phil. Trans.*, 1865.   [3] *Il Nuovo Cimento*, vii. 321.

The system of atomic weights most generally adopted at the present day takes hydrogen as unity, though unfortunately there is not a universal agreement as to this matter, for a considerable number of chemists prefer to use the round number 16 for oxygen, on the ground that if this number is used instead of the somewhat smaller value which more exactly represents the atomic weight of oxygen when hydrogen is taken as the unit, the atomic weights of many of the more common of the elements may also be represented by whole numbers without appreciable error. Thus, if O is 16, we have $As = 75$, $Br = 80$, $Ca = 40$, $C = 12$, $F = 19$, $Fe = 56$, $I = 127$, $Hg = 200$, $N = 14$, $P = 31$, $Na = 23$, $S = 32$, $Sn = 119$, very approximately. It must not be forgotten, however, that if $O = 16$, the value $1\cdot008$ must be assigned for all exact purposes to hydrogen. Quite recently a committee of the German Chemical Society has drawn up a table of atomic weights in accordance with the best available evidence, in which they recommend the use of the number 16 for oxygen, and $1\cdot01$ for hydrogen, as sufficiently near for all practical purposes.

Whether the one scale or the other is used, however, is a matter of small importance in comparison with the immense advantages which have accrued from a general agreement as to the methods by which the atomic weights may be calculated from the chemical equivalents. As a consequence of this agreement certain relations among the numerical values of the atomic weights have been discovered, and the nature of the elements themselves set in an entirely new light (see next chapter).

It seems proper to recall at this point the names of a few of the more prominent among the workers who have laboured to introduce accuracy into the experimental estimations of the combining proportions of the elements, from which the atomic weights of the same are, as already explained, derived. The first to make experiments explicitly directed towards the estimation of the relative weights of atoms was, of course, John Dalton, but the numbers he obtained were in many cases so far from the truth, that his results have at the present day no interest, except from the historical point of view. The same may be said of the "equivalents" calculated later by Wollaston (*Phil. Trans.*, 1814), and the first chemist to whom science is indebted for estimating these ratios with a tolerable approach to accuracy was the Swedish professor Berzelius (born 1779, died 1848). To this business, indeed, he devoted the greater part of a laborious life. His example was to a certain extent followed, and a number of very exact estimations were due to the labours of Dumas, Pelouze, De Marignac, and others. Later, the most eminent among the numerous workers in this field was J. S. Stas, who, in a series of papers of which the first was published in 1860, gave the results of his experiments on the atomic weights of ten elements, conducted with precautions more elaborate, and with a skill more refined than anything previously known in researches of this kind.[1]

The object aimed at is to determine exactly the proportion of each element which enters into combination with the unit weight of some one element taken as the standard. During the first quarter of this century oxygen was used as the standard for comparison, and its combining unit was assumed to be 100. But inasmuch as hydrogen enters into combination in the smallest proportion of all, it was soon found more convenient to take hydrogen as the standard, and refer all other combining weights to that of hydrogen, assumed to be 1. The hypothesis suggested by Prout in 1815, that the atomic weights of the elements are multiples of the atomic weight of hydrogen by whole numbers, doubtless assisted in promoting the adoption of hydrogen as the unit. This hypothesis in its original form has long since been abandoned.

The methods actually employed for the purpose contemplated are very diverse. It is not possible in all cases to obtain compounds of the elements with hydrogen. The metals, for example, afford but few examples of such compounds. On the other hand, the metals form oxides which, as a class, are remarkably definite and stable substances. Analytical difficulties

[1] A complete account of the object, scope, and results of Stas' work is given in the Memorial Lecture by Professor J. W. Mallet, read before the Chemical Society, Dec. 1892.—*Trans. Chem. Soc.*, lxiii. 1 (1893).

of a practical kind, however, also stand in the way of directly ascertaining the proportions of the elements in such compounds, and chemists resort, therefore, to the chlorides, bromides, sulphates, and other compounds, as well as to the direct examination of the hydrides or oxides for the information desired. The ratio in which hydrogen and oxygen stand to each other in water is a matter of such fundamental importance, and the experimental processes employed are so instructive, that a short account of them may be given here.

All the early determinations of the composition of water by weight were based upon the fact that copper oxide may be heated to redness by itself without decomposition or loss of weight, but that in presence of hydrogen it yields copper, which remains behind, and water in vapour, which may be condensed and collected in suitable apparatus, so that its weight can be determined. Hence the loss of weight sustained by oxide of copper heated in a stream of pure hydrogen would give the weight of oxygen in the water which is formed. The difference between the weight of water and that of the oxygen in it gives the hydrogen. The first results of real value were obtained by Dumas, and were published in 1842.

The figure, given in Dumas' paper in the *Annales de Chimie*, shows the vessel in which hydrogen was generated, tubes containing materials for purifying and drying the gas, a bulb containing pure cupric oxide, and a second bulb with connected tubes, in which the water formed is collected without loss of vapour, carried away by the escaping excess of hydrogen. The weight of the bulb containing the oxide is determined with great care before the experiment begins, and again at its close. The weight of the bulb and of the connected tubes is also determined when empty, and after the collection of the water. Many precautions are necessary, and many were actually adopted by Dumas, but all sources of error could not be avoided at that day, even if they were recognised. Some of the experimental difficulties are obvious enough, such as the impurities present in hydrogen obtained by the customary methods, the difficulty of removing moisture from the gas, and the intrusion of air by leakage through the joints of the apparatus, the presence of impurities in the copper oxide, the uncertainty of the weighings performed in atmospheric air, the condition of which as to moisture, pressure, and temperature varies from day to day. These and others, unsuspected in Dumas' time, such as the retention of hydrogen by the reduced metallic copper, have been considered, and more or less completely met by later investigations. The results of these successive inquiries into the application of this method are given below:—

Names of Experimenters.	Combining Weight of Oxygen.	Probable Error.
Dumas	15·9607	± ·0070
Erdmann and Marchand	15·975	± ·0113
Cook and Richards	15·869	± ·0020
Keiser	15·9514	± ·0011
Dittmar and Henderson	15·8667	± ·0046

An entirely distinct method, involving the difficult task of uniting oxygen to hydrogen, and weighing not only the water produced, but the gases themselves before combination, was undertaken by Professor E. W. Morley. The hydrogen was absorbed by palladium, and the metal with the "occluded" gas weighed separately. The oxygen was weighed in the gaseous form in compensated globes, and the combination of the hydrogen with the oxygen was effected by means of electric sparks, in an apparatus in which the resulting water could be collected and weighed, while the unconsumed residue, whether of hydrogen or oxygen, could be collected apart and determined. The result of a series of such experiments gave for the combining weight the value

$$15\cdot 8790 \pm \cdot 00028.$$

One other important method, involving again a different principle, must not be omitted: this is a comparison of the densities of the two gases, hydrogen and oxygen, with the assumption, fully justified by abundant evidence which cannot be discussed at this point, that supposing them to be true gases (see Chapter IX.), their densities would be proportional to their combining weights. Oxygen and hydrogen are not, however, perfect gases, uniting in the exact ratio of one volume to two volumes. As the combined result of very elaborate experiments conducted by Dr. Alexander Scott[1] and by E. W.

[1] *Phil. Trans.*, 1893.

Morley,[1] the ratio is actually 1 to 2·0028, with a small probable error. This fact has to be taken into account in estimating the chemical combining weight of the gases from their relative densities.

A large number of weighings of these gases have been made by successive generations of chemists from the times of Cavendish and Lavoisier onwards, but the first determinations which attained to any considerable degree of accuracy were those made by Regnault about 1845. The subject has been taken up again in recent years by Lord Rayleigh,[2] and by Morley, whose work has already been referred to, also by the late Professor J. P. Cooke, and others; the result being that the number finally adopted, as expressing the density of oxygen, is appreciably less than the number resulting from Regnault's and the other earlier estimations. In the end the results stand as follows: the value of the symbol O from the synthesis of water is 15·8796; from the densities of the gases it is 15·8769. The number 15·88 may therefore be taken for all practical purposes as the combining proportion of oxygen.[3]

---

[1] *Amer. Journ. Sci.* [3], xli. 220, 276.

[2] "On the Densities of the Principal Gases" (*Proc. Roy. Soc.*, liii. 134).

[3] These are the values calculated by Professor F. W. Clarke from all the best data combined. See "Smithsonian Constants of Nature. A Recalculation of the Atomic Weights," 1897.

CHAPTER IV

NUMERICAL RELATIONS AMONG THE ATOMIC WEIGHTS: CLASSIFICATION OF THE ELEMENTS

It may be inferred, from what has been stated in the preceding chapter, that the process of determining an atomic weight resolves itself into two parts, namely, the exact determination of the combining proportion, or, as it was formerly called, the equivalent, and the multiplication of the equivalent by a factor, 1, 2, 3, or 4, derived from the application of the law of Avogadro, the law of Dulong and Petit, or from some other consideration, according to the circumstances of the case.

A complete digest of all the determinations of modern times has been prepared by Professor F. W. Clarke, and published as a volume of the "Constants of Nature," by the Smithsonian Institution, Washington, and the numbers adopted by Professor Clarke will be used in the discussion which occupies the latter part of this chapter. Some of these values are obviously inexact, but they represent the best estimate which can be made in the present state of knowledge.

The hypothesis put forward by Prout early in the century has been a fruitful source of discussion, and even at the present day is regarded by some chemists as hardly yet disposed of. Prout supposed that the atomic weights of the elements are multiples by whole numbers of the atomic weight of hydrogen; but in consequence of the atomic weight of chlorine, according to the experiments of many chemists, invariably coming out midway between 35 and 36, it is obvious that the principle thus expressed is untenable. Consequently it was suggested, first, that the hypothesis might be modified by making one half the atomic weight of hydrogen, and subsequently one fourth the atomic weight of that element, the unit. Stas began his researches with a strong prepossession in favour of Prout's hypothesis, but the results of his protracted labours, by far the most trustworthy of all the experimental investigations of the subject which we possess, have only tended to render it more improbable that any such relation among the atomic weights really subsists.

A large part of the interest attaching to this subject arises from its association with the question as to the probable nature and origin of the chemical elements. On the one hand, each of the elementary bodies may represent a separate creation independent of all the rest, and having nothing in common with them. On the other hand, supposing a relation can be traced between the masses of the atoms of which different elements are composed, then it is open to inquiry whether they may not have had a common origin; whether they may not represent several stages in a formative or evolutionary process, operating upon a primitive simple material; and whether in that case it may not be possible to transform one into another by the operation of agencies within the range of practicable experiment.

It had long been noticed, and specially pointed out by Döbereiner in 1829, that when families of closely allied elements are examined they are commonly found to consist of three members, for example chlorine, bromine, iodine or sulphur, selenion, tellurium or lithium, sodium, potassium; and that in such cases the values of the atomic weights are so related that the middle term of the series is nearly the arithmetical mean of the two other terms. For example:—

$$Na = 23 = \frac{Li + K}{2} = \frac{7 + 39}{2}$$

But no general discussion of the subject possessing much interest appeared until 1858, when Dumas published a most interesting *Mémoire sur les Équivalents des Corps Simples.*[1]

In this memoir Dumas drew attention to the analogy which may be recognised between series of closely related elements and the known series of compound radicles, such as methyl, ethyl, propyl, &c., of which so many examples occur among carbon compounds. Thus, regarding hydrogen as the first member of the series, and writing equivalent quantities

[1] *Ann. Chim. Phys.* [3], lv. 129.

of the hydrocarbon radicles in succession with their combining weights, we have—

Hydrogen	H	1
Methyl	CH_3	15
Ethyl	C_2H_5	29
Propyl	C_3H_7	43
Butyl	C_4H_9	57
Amyl	C_5H_{11}	71
&c.	&c.	&c.

Here it is obvious that in passing from term to term there is a common difference of 14 units, and representing the value of the first term as a, and the difference as d, the value of any single term may be expressed by $a + nd$. Hence, on taking three terms at equal distances in the series, it is found that the combining weight of the intermediate term is the arithmetical mean of the combining weights of the other two. For example, 43 is equal to the sum of 29 and 57 divided by 2. Dumas also drew attention to the fact that in such a series combining proportions represented by such numbers as 141 and 281, 127 and 253, stand so nearly in the relation of 1 to 2 that if they belonged to substances supposed to be elementary, and not known to be compound, it would almost certainly be inferred that this actually represented the ratio of the one to the other. Relations very similar to these are traceable among the members of the several recognised natural families of the elements, and Dumas was able, with the atomic weights accepted at that time, many of which had been corrected by his own experiments, to represent several series by formulæ of this kind. He further showed that, on placing certain of these groups side by side, a common difference ran through the successive terms of the parallel series. For example :—

Fluorine, F . . 19	Nitrogen, N . . 14
Chlorine, Cl . . 35·5	Phosphorus, P. . 31
Bromine, Br . . 80	Arsenic, As. . . 75
Iodine, I . . . 127	Antimony, Sb . . 122

Here the difference between each term of the halogens and the corresponding member of the nitrogen series is, with one exception, exactly 5. Later determinations have, however, so modified these numbers that the difference is no longer constant throughout. The question of the numerical relations among the atomic weights was not long suffered to remain at rest. Many writers had drawn attention to various cases of individual or serial peculiarities, but so long as the atomic weights of the elements remained uncoördinated with a common standard, it is obvious that no substantial progress could be made. We have seen in the last chapter how, by the recognition of the law of Avogadro and of the law of Dulong and Petit, the atomic weights were ultimately systematised; and almost so soon as this was accomplished a very remarkable discovery was made, which ultimately brought the whole of the known elements within one comprehensive scheme. This scheme, which is usually incorrectly referred to as the "periodic law," is based upon a principle which would more appropriately receive that designation. The principle which is now generally recognised may be expressed as follows: *If the elements are arranged in the order of the numerical value of their atomic weights, their properties, physical and chemical, vary in a recurrent or periodic manner.*

We will now endeavour to trace the successive steps which have led up to this generalisation. The existence of triads of closely related elements, as already stated, had long been recognised; and an extension of this idea, recalling the properties of homologous series, had been discussed by Dumas, with results already described. But the various series of elements remained as separate series, disconnected one from another.[1]

[1] A claim has been put forward by Messieurs Lecoq de Boisbaudran and Lapparent in favour of A. E. B. de Chancourtois, for a share in the credit of having originated the idea of the periodic relation of properties to atomic weights among the chemical elements. In 1862–63 M. de Chancourtois, a geologist and engineer, presented a series of papers to the French Académie des Sciences, which were collected together in 1863 under one title, "Le Vis Tellurique, classement naturel des corps simples ou radicaux obtenu au moyen d'un Système de Classification helicoidal et numerique." By coiling a helix with an angle of 45° round a cylinder divided vertically into sixteen equal parts by lines drawn from the circular base, the helix cuts these lines at equal distances in its ascent, and the points of intersection were supposed to represent the atomic weights of elements which differed from one another by 16, or multiples of 16. The author seems to have had a dim idea that properties were in some way related to atomic weight, but this idea is so confused by fantastic notions of his own, that it is impossible to be sure that he really recognised anything like periodicity in this relation.

In July 1864 a paper was communicated to the *Chemical News* by Mr. John A. R. Newlands, in which, in the course of discussing certain supposed regularities in the atomic weights of the elements, he drew up a list of all the then known elements in the order of the numerical value of their atomic weights, and in the month following he was led to announce, with reference to this table, the existence of a simple relation among the elements so arranged. Numbering the elements in order, hydrogen 1, lithium 2, glucinum 3, boron 4, and so on, he pointed out that "the eighth element, starting from a given one, was a sort of repetition of the first, or that elements belonging to the same group stood to each other in a relation similar to that between the extremes of one or more octaves in music."

Almost immediately after this, namely, in October of the same year, an interesting paper appeared in the *Quarterly Journal of Science* (vol. i. p. 642), by Dr. Odling, on "The Proportional Numbers of the Elements," in which he pointed to the marked continuity in the arithmetical series, resulting from an arrangement of the whole of the then known elements in the order of their atomic weights, or "proportional numbers," as he preferred to call them, the only exceptions to the very gradual increase in value of the consecutive terms being manifested between the numbers 40 and 50 (Ca and Ti), 65 and 75 (Zn and As), 96 and 104 (Mo and Ro), 138 and 184 (Ta and W), 184 and

195 (W and Nb), and 210 and 231·5 (Bi and Th).[1] In this paper Odling showed that this purely arithmetical seriation may be made to agree with an arrangement of the elements according to their generally recognised affinities, and he drew up a table, of which the following is a revised version, published in Watts' Dictionary of Chemistry (vol. iii. p. 975), only a few months later:—

						Mo	96	W	184
							—	Au	196·5
						Pd	106·5	Pt	197
L	7	Na	23		—	Ag	108		—
G	9	Mg	24	Zn	65	Cd	112	Hg	200
B	11	Al	27·5		—		—	Tl	203
C	12	Si	28		—	Sn	118	Pb	207
N	14	P	31	As	75	Sb	122	Bi	210
O	16	S	32	Se	79·5	Te	129		—
F	19	Cl	35·5	Br	80	Te	127		—
		K	39	Rb	85	Cs	133		
		Ca	40	Sr	87·5	Ba	137		
		Ti	48	Zr	89·5		—	Th	231
		Cr	52·5		—	V	138		
		Mn	55		—		—		

Here manganese stands proxy for the iron metals, and platinum and palladium for their respective congeners.

Towards the end of this paper, the author drew attention to the large number of instances in which

---

[1] Most of these breaks are now accounted for by the existence of elements discovered since that time, viz. Sc=44, Ga=69, and Ge=72; the earth metals, La=137, Ce=139, Neo-dymium=Nd =140, Praseo-dymium=Pr=142, Sm=149, Tb=159, Eb=165, while Ta is now 181, and Nb 94 (?).

the atomic weights of proximate elements differ from one another by 48 or 44, or 40 or 16, and remarks: "We cannot help looking wistfully at the number 4 as embodying, somehow or other, the unit of a common difference."[1] From this it would appear that something analogous to the idea of homology, which had attracted Dumas, was hovering in his mind. In conclusion, the pregnant observation occurs that "among the members of every well-defined group, the sequence of properties and sequence of atomic weights are strictly parallel to one another."

In August 1865 Mr. Newlands again wrote to the *Chemical News* (vol. xii. p. 83), as follows: "If the elements are arranged in the order of their equivalents, with a few slight transpositions, as in the accompanying table, it will be observed that elements belonging to the same group usually appear in the same horizontal line.

	No.		No.		No.		No.		No.		No.		No.		No.
H	1	F	8	Cl	15	Co & Ni	22	Br	. 29	Pd	36	I	. 42	Pt & Ir	50
Li	2	Na	9	K	16	Cu	. 23	Rb	. 30	Ag	37	Cs	. 44	Tl	. 53
G	3	Mg	10	Ca	17	Zn	. 25	Sr	. 31	Cd	38	Ba & V	45	Pb	. 54
Bo	4	Al	11	Cr	19	Y	. 24	Ce & La	33	U	40	Ta	. 46	Th	. 56
C	5	Si	12	Ti	18	In	. 26	Zr	. 32	Sn	39	W	. 47	Hg	. 52
N	6	P	13	Mn	20	As	. 27	Di & Mo	34	Sb	41	Nb	. 48	Bi	. 55
O	7	S	14	Fe	21	Se	. 28	Ro & Ru	35	Te	43	Au	. 49	Os	. 51

Note.—When two elements happen to have the same equivalent, both are designated by the same number.

---

[1] From the more exact values for the atomic weights to be given later, it will be seen that these differences are but roughly represented by these whole numbers.

It will also be seen that the numbers of analogous elements generally differ either by 7 or by some multiple of 7; in other words, members of the same group stand to each other in the same relation as the extremities of one or more octaves in music. This relationship Newlands proposed to call the "Law of Octaves."

The following year the same chemist brought the relations which he had observed to the notice of the Chemical Society of London, and produced a table similar to the above, with a few alterations, by which mercury was brought into the same line with cadmium, lead into the same line with tin. He also used atomic weights calculated on Cannizzaro's system, so far as known facts would permit. The time, however, had not arrived for the general acceptance of ideas of this kind, obscured as they necessarily were by imperfect knowledge, both of atomic weights and of the inter-relations of the elements as to properties. The Chemical Society in 1866 were disposed to laugh at Newlands and his "law." Twenty-one years later the Royal Society awarded him the Davy Medal for his discovery.

Others, however, soon took up the question in a very serious spirit, and with less of the hesitation which had characterised the treatment of the subject up to this time. This arose concurrently with a feeling of greater confidence in the revised system of atomic weights, which by the end of the decade 1860–70 were quite generally adopted, at any rate in England and Germany; and probably out of this confidence was gradually developed some idea that the relations already noticed did indeed correspond to some profound physical law relating to the nature of the elements. In March 1869, Professor D. Mendeléeff communicated a paper to the Russian Chemical Society,[1] in which he set out an arrangement of the elements in a table having considerable resemblance to the table drawn up by Odling five years before.

MENDELÉEF'S TABLE OF THE ELEMENTS, 1869.

			Ti = 50	Zr = 90	? = 180
			V = 51	Nb = 94	Ta = 182
			Cr = 52	Mo = 96	W = 186
			Mn = 55	Rh = 104·4	Pt = 197·4
			Fe = 56	Ru = 104·4	Ir = 198
		Ni =	Co = 59	Pd = 106·6	Os = 199
H = 1			Cu = 63·4	Ag = 108	Hg = 200
	Be = 9·4	Mg = 24	Zn = 65·2	Cd = 112	
	B = 11	Al = 27·4	? = 68	Ur = 116	Au = 197 ?
	C = 12	Si = 28	? = 70	Sn = 118	
	N = 14	P = 31	As = 75	Sb = 122	Bi = 210
	O = 16	S = 32	Se = 79·4	Te = 128 ?	
	F = 19	Cl = 35·5	Br = 80	I = 127	
Li = 7	Na = 23	K = 39	Rb = 85·4	Cs = 133	Tl = 204
		Ca = 40	Sr = 87·6	Ba = 137	Pb = 207
		? = 45	Ce = 92		
		? Er = 56	La = 94		
		? Yt = 60	Di = 95		
		? In = 75·6	Th = 118 ?		

In commenting upon this table the German abstract,[1] which is alone accessible to English, and presumably also to most German readers, represents the author's view by the following words:

[1] *Zeitschrift für Chemie*, 1869, p. 405.

" 1. Die nach der Grösse des Atomgewichts geordneten Elemente zeigen eine Stufenweise Abänderung in den Eigenschaften." This appears to contain an important error of translation, for Mendeléeff, in a communication made to the Berlin Chemical Society [1] upon the history of the question, explains in a footnote that the word which in the Russian original means *periodische*, has been rendered *stufenweise* (gradual, or by degrees). It must, however, be remarked that the table does not so obviously suggest periodicity of properties in the elements so arranged, as does Newlands' earlier, though confessedly imperfect, attempt.

In this paper Mendeléeff pointed out that the discovery and properties of elements then unknown, as for example analogues of silicon and aluminium, might be predicted; and further expressed the conviction that such a system might be applied to the correction of atomic weights, citing as an example the case of tellurium, which, according to this view, ought to have an atomic weight smaller than that of iodine.

In December 1869, Lothar Meyer, then professor in the Polytechnicum at Carlsruhe, contributed a paper to Liebig's *Annalen*,[2] entitled "Die Natur der Chemischen Elemente als Function ihrer Atomgewichte," in which, after giving a table of elements, with their atomic weights, which he described as

---

[1] *Berichte der Deutsch Chem. Ges.*, iv. 351 (1871).
[2] Supplement, vi. and vii., 1870, p. 354.

substantially identical with that of Mendeléeff, he pointed out that from the table it may be deduced that the properties of the elements are generally a *periodic function* of the atomic weight. This observation seems to show that the periodicity did not become apparent to Meyer, at any rate, till the table of Mendeléeff had been subjected to the modifications adopted by him, and shown below :—

I.	II.	III.	IV.	V.	VI.	VII.	VIII.	IX.
	B 11	Al 27·3				?In 113·4		Tl 202·7
	C 12	Si 28				Sn 117·8		Pb 206·4
	N 14	P 30·9	Ti 48	As 74·9	Zr 89·7	Sb 122·1		Bi 207·5
	O 16	S 32	V 51·2	Sc 78	Nb 93·7	Te 128?	Ta 182·2	
	F 19·1	Cl 35·4	Cr 52·4	Br 79·75	Mo 95·6	I 126·5	W 183·5	
			Mn 54·8		Ru 103·5		Os 198·6?	
			Fe 55·9		Rh 104·1		Ir 196·7	
			Co= Ni 58·6		Pd 106·2		Pt 196·7	
Li 7·0	Na 22·9	K 39	Cu 63·3	Rb 85·2	Ag 107·7	Cs 132·7	Au 192·2	
?Be 9·3	Mg 23·9	Ca 39·9	Zn 64·9	Sr 87	Cd 111·6	Ba 136·8	Hg 199·8	

Obviously in this scheme the same or similar properties recur when the atomic weight is increased by a certain amount, which is first 16, then about 46, and afterwards amounts to 88 to 92 units. This had been noticed by Odling and others previously, but Meyer got a step further when he pointed out (*loc. cit.* p. 388) that the combining capacity of the atoms rises and falls regularly and equally in two such series as the following :—

Univalent.	Biv.	Triv.	Quadriv.	Triv.	Biv.	Univ.
Li	Be	B	C	N	O	F
Na	Mg	Al	Si	P	S	Cl

A complete and triumphant vindication of the principle of periodicity is provided by the graphic representation of the relation of atomic volume to atomic weight, drawn up for the first time by Meyer at the end of this paper. The diagram he gave, and of which a portion is reproduced on the opposite page, speaks for itself.

It is evident, then, that the conception of the periodic relation gradually and independently took shape in the mind of more than one chemist during the period we have had under review. But it would be only just to point out that a depth of conviction, which almost amounts to inspiration, carried Mendeléeff further in the study and application of the principle than any of his predecessors or contemporaries. In August 1871 he drew up a complete exposition[1] of the principle, which he henceforth calls the *periodic law*, and of the deductions which may be made from it. And here for the first time appeared the table which, in some form or other, is now to be found in the pages of nearly every text-book of theoretical chemistry, and which is now employed as the most generally received basis of classification of the elements. The table is reproduced in this original form in order to show how great an advance it represents in the development of the fundamental idea.

[1] *Annalen*, Supplem., viii. p. 133 (1872).

Series.	Group I. R_2O	Group II. RO	Group III. R_2O_3	Group IV. RH_4 RO_2	Group V. RH_3 R_2O_5	Group VI. RH_2 RO_3	Group VII. RH R_2O_7	Group VIII. — RO_4
1	H =1							
2	Li =7	Be=9·4	B =11	C =12	N =14	O =16	F =19	
3	Na=23	Mg=24	Al=27·3	Si =28	P =31	S =32	Cl =35·5	
4	K =39	Ca=40	— =44	Ti =48	V =51	Cr =52	Mn=55	Fe =56 Co =59 Ni =59 Cu =63
5	(Cu=63)	Zn =65	— =68	— =72	As=75	Se=78	Br=80	
6	Rb=85	Sr =87	?Yt=88	Zr =90	Nb=94	Mo=96	— =100	Ru=104 Rh=104 Pd =106 Ag=108
7	(Ag=108)	Cd =112	In =113	Sn=118	Sb=122	Te=125	I =127	
8	Cs =133	Ba=137	?Di=138	?Ce=140				
9	(—)							
10	…		?Er =178	?La=180	Ta =182	W =184		Os =195 Ir =197 Pt =198 Au=199
11	(Au=199)	Hg=200	Tl =204	Pb=207	Bi =208			
12				Th =231		U =240		

In connection with the discussion of this scheme, Mendeléeff's most brilliant achievement was its application to the prediction of the properties of elements yet to be discovered. "When," he says, in one of the characteristic footnotes in his "Principles of Chemistry" (vol. ii. p. 25), "in 1871 I wrote a paper on the application of the periodic law to the determination of the properties of yet undiscovered elements, I did not think I should live to see the verification of this consequence of the law, but such was to be the case. Three elements were described, eka-boron, eka-aluminium, and eka-silicon; and now, after the lapse of twenty years, I have had the great pleasure of seeing them discovered and named after those countries where the rare minerals containing them are found, and where they were discovered—Gallia, Scandinavia, and Germany." Mendeléeff's eka-boron has been called by Nilson, its discoverer, Scandium; the representative of eka-aluminium was discovered in the zinc-blende of the Pyrenees by Lecoq de Boisbaudran in 1875, and named Gallium; while a new silver ore at Freiberg yielded, in the hands of Clemens Winkler, a new metal, which he recognised as the representative of eka-silicon, and to which he patriotically gave the name Germanium.

The process which led Mendeléeff to this remarkable result consists, naturally, in the careful study of the properties, not only of the series in which the unoccupied place occurred, but also of the properties of the neighbouring series, and of their mutual relations. A few facts may be given to show the nature of the conclusions to which he was led in one case, and the extent to which they were afterwards justified.

To eka-silicon Mendeléeff assigned, in 1871, the atomic weight 72. He described it as a difficultly fusible, dark grey, metallic substance, which in the state of powder would pass at a red heat into the difficultly fusible oxide EsO_2. The specific gravity of the oxide would be about 4·7, and similar in appearance, perhaps in crystalline form, to titanic oxide. The metal would act on steam only with difficulty, and on acids slightly, though more easily on alkalis, while the oxide would display more decided acidifying power than titanic oxide. The fluoride, EsF_4, would be volatile, but not gaseous at common temperatures. The chloride, $EsCl_4$, would be a volatile liquid, boiling at a temperature about 100°, probably somewhat lower; and there would be a tetrethide, $EsEt_4$, with a boiling point about 160°.

Germanium is described as a greyish white, lustrous, very brittle metal, which melts at about 900°, and crystallises in regular octahedrons on cooling. It is unchanged in air at ordinary temperatures, but is oxidised when heated in a state of powder. It dissolves in sulphuric acid, but not in hydrochloric acid. The oxide, GeO_2, is a dense white powder of specific gravity 4·7, slightly soluble in water, producing a solution which has a sour taste. The oxide dissolves readily in alkalis. The fluoride is a volatile substance, probably solid. The chloride, $GeCl_4$, is a colourless liquid, which boils at 86°, and the tetrethide, $GeEt_4$, is a liquid which boils at 160°. The atomic weight of germanium is 71·93 when $H = 1$.

That the periodic system of the elements stands for something which is actually based on natural physical relations, no one can now be supposed to doubt. It brings into view a number of facts in the chemical history of the elements which would otherwise be less apparent, and it does undoubtedly support very strongly the idea that all the elements included in Mendeléeff's and Meyer's synopsis belong to one system of things, and perhaps have common constituents, or may have arisen from a common origin. Nevertheless, such a synopsis is encumbered with some difficulties, which have not yet been satisfactorily accounted for. The fundamental idea of the scheme is the periodic "law," which asserts that the properties of the elements are dependent upon their atomic weights. If that were strictly true, the existence of two elements having the same atomic weight, but different properties, would be impossible. Hence the relations of such elements as cobalt and nickel, ruthenium and rhodium, are far from clear in the original table. And even if we substitute for the round numbers used by Mendeléeff in 1871 the values for the atomic weight which result from all the best recorded experiments, so that these coincidences cease to be exact, the difficulty still remains that several elements—iron, nickel, cobalt, ruthenium, rhodium, palladium, osmium, iridium, platinum—are not provided for. In some cases the peculiarities of individual elements, and their relations to others, could never have been suspected from their position in the table. The case of thallium is one of the most notable. This metal has a very strong resemblance to lead, but its sulphate, and several other salts, are entirely unlike the corresponding compounds of lead, but, on the other hand, agree closely in characters with the compounds of the alkali metals. Lead itself stands in a similar relation to the metals of the alkaline earths. The positions of thallium and lead in the table would scarcely have suggested these characters, if these two elements had been previously unknown. And now we have the newly discovered helium, argon, and the rest, with their extraordinary characteristic of chemical inactivity, which marks them off from all other known substances, elementary or compound, and of which no prognostication is to be found in the almost innumerable memoirs relating to the atomic weights of the elements published previously to the discovery of argon. It must of course be remembered, however, that since the discovery of argon and helium, the gases of the atmosphere and those obtained from minerals have been submitted by Ramsay to a special search, with the object of discovering other elements of intermediate and higher atomic weight, and his labour has been rewarded by the recognition of neon, metargon, and krypton, as already mentioned. But the endeavour to introduce these new substances into the periodic scheme has, up to the present, been but imperfectly successful; for such arrangements as the figure of eight proposed by Crookes[1] involve some violence to natural associations, hydrogen, for example, being separated from all the metals, and made the first member of a group in which the halogens follow.

Another point is worthy of notice in a discussion of these figures. The numerical amount of the differences observable between elements which are consecutive in the list vary very much. The smallest difference appears to lie between nickel and cobalt, and to be equal to about $0·25$; while there are many cases where the difference amounts to between 4 and 5 units or more, as, for example, $Cu - Co = 4·63$, $Sn - In = 5·16$, $Cs - I = 6·00$, and, $Rb - Br = 5·44$. In the last case it may be that the newly discovered krypton stands between, with an atomic weight about 80. The point, however, is that the transition from the even to the odd series, as, for example, from fluorine to sodium, or from chlorine to potassium, or from bromine to rubidium, is not marked by a difference noticeably greater, or less, than is observable in many other parts of the list of elements. The ninth series in Mendeléeff's table will doubtless be filled up by many of the elements

---

[1] *Proc. Roy. Soc.*, lxiii. 408 (1898).

derived from the so-called Swedish or rare earths. The atomic weights of some of these have already been determined with sufficient show of probability to allow of their finding provisional places in the table. Among these may be mentioned neodymium 139·7, praseodymium 142·5, samarium 149·1, gadolinium 155·6, terbium 158·8, erbium 165·0, thulium 169·4, ytterbium 171·9.

From all that has gone before, it may readily be supposed that many speculations have been put forward as to the origin of the elements, or in explanation of their assumed complex nature. Of these, one of the most serious, though by no means the earliest, is embodied in a paper communicated to the British Association by the late Professor Carnelley.[1] It is typical of a whole group of these speculative compositions, but is more carefully worked out than many of the rest. The author proceeds upon the assumption of *at least* two primal elements, A and B, which, by their combination in various proportions, give masses approximately equal to the atomic weights of the known elements, which are regarded as analogous to hydrocarbon radicles; but even this scheme, attractive as it is on the whole, requires us to assume for B a *negative* weight equal to something between $-1·99$ and $-2·00$. It cannot be forgotten that a somewhat similar device

---

[1] "Suggestions as to the cause of the Periodic Law and the Nature of the Chemical Elements."—*British Association*, 1885; *Chemical News*, 1886.

was the last refuge of the declining theory of phlogiston more than a century ago.

There seems to be a general disposition at the present time to revive and rehabilitate the ancient notion of the unity of matter, and its derivation from a common *prothyl* (πρώτη, first; ὕλη, stuff or matter).

> "All things the world which fill
> Of but one stuff are spun."

This idea has been made the text of an interesting address by Sir William Crookes, on the "Genesis of the Chemical Elements."[1] It has also for many years been the guiding principle of a remarkable series of researches, by Sir Norman Lockyer, on the spectroscopy of the sun and stars. According to Lockyer, the elements, as known to terrestrial chemistry, are more or less completely dissociated into substances of simpler constitution at the high temperatures prevailing in these bodies and their gaseous atmospheres. It seems fully established that the greater number of the lines exhibited by the spectra of common metals, such as iron, calcium, manganese, are wanting in the spectra of the hotter stars; while a small number of such lines remain, accompanied by other lines not recognisable as belonging to any known terrestrial element. And when the spectra of certain stars are ranged in the order of what is supposed to be ascending tempera-

[1] *British Association Reports*, 1886.

ture in the series of stars, there is a progressive disappearance of the old, and appearance of the new lines, corresponding to this progressive dissociation. What is much needed, is some experimental evidence that dissociation of the elements does actually occur at the high temperatures now obtainable under laboratory conditions.

The association of the ultimate particles of prothyl must be supposed to be accomplished by a process comparable with that which in ordinary chemistry is called "polymerisation." This implies the association together of a number of particles, elementary or compound, into groups. No consideration, based on the extreme minuteness of atoms,[1] need deter us from admitting such a conception; because, after all, what we call *size*, great or small, is relative only to the range of human measurements. But if there is any objection to the introduction of the idea into serious physics, it will probably be found in the relations of some of the atomic ratios, commonly called atomic weights. It is usually conceded that the atomic weights of silver and chlorine, for example, have been determined with very great accuracy, the probable error

---

[1] The estimate of Lord Kelvin, though familiar, may be recalled to the recollection of the reader: "Imagine a globe of water, or glass, as large as a football (or say a globe of 16 centimetres diameter), to be magnified up to the size of the earth, each constituent molecule being magnified in the same proportion. The magnified structure would be more coarse-grained than a heap of small shot, but probably less coarse-grained than a heap of footballs."—*Lecture at Royal Inst.*, Feb. 1883.

being less than 1 part in 10,000. Taking the ratio between these two, as given by Stas, to be

$$\text{Ag} : \text{Cl} :: 107\cdot930 : 35\cdot457,$$

there is no common measure for these two numbers, nor can any two numbers near to them be found having a common measure, unless they are altered by addition or subtraction of amounts much greater than the experimental error. Suppose even such round numbers as 108 and 35·5 be taken, there is no common measure for them greater than ·5; and if these two forms of matter be assumed to be made up of the same "prothyl," the number of units of such primordial stuff required to compose one atom of chlorine and of silver, would be at least 355 and 1080 respectively. On this ground alone it would be difficult to find any known mechanical principle to account for the formation of such a highly stable thing as an atom of silver, by the congregation of 1080 equal and similar particles. And supposing this difficulty got over, another at once presents itself as to the nature of the primitive particles: are these really *atoms*, that is indivisibles, or does not a similar hypothesis seem to be required to account for their existence? Thus visions of sub-atoms of sub-atoms seem to arise in the mind, suggestive of hypotheses worthy only of a Ptolemaic philosophy.

The alternatives seem to lie between the Boscovichian doctrine of centres of force, which cannot be discussed here, and the theory of vortices, which we owe to Lord Kelvin. Fascinating as is the idea of a universal frictionless fluid, in which vortices of variously knotted forms subsist for ever, inalterable and indestructible, and yield to our senses and instruments all those effects which we ascribe to matter, the theory in its application to chemistry has not yet been brought into harmony with all the facts. But supposing such a theory to be accepted, one consequence would be that the present notion of the dissociability of the chemical elements would have to be put aside, for each kind of vortex would represent a special creative act which could not be undone. There would be, similarly, an end of transmutation of one element into another, and to some extent also of the supposed significance of atomic weights.[1]

In such a position it is the duty and the best interest of the chemist to preserve a perfectly unbiassed mind, and to pursue the safer path of experimental inquiry.

[1] Mr. J. Larmor has recently propounded an "Electro-dynamical Theory of the Electric and Luminiferous Medium," which gives a new view of inter-atomic action, and the nature of the ether.— *Phil. Trans.*, 1897, 205.

CHAPTER V

ORIGIN AND DEVELOPMENT OF THE IDEAS OF
VALENCY AND THE LINKING OF ATOMS

It has already been explained in Chapter III. that the discovery by Dumas of the fact that chlorine may be introduced into organic compounds in exchange for hydrogen, equivalent for equivalent, led to very important changes in the then current ideas of chemical combination. Up to that time the electro-chemical theory of Berzelius had been almost entirely predominant, and, naturally, the notion that an electro-negative element like chlorine could be exchanged for an electro-positive element such as hydrogen, without fundamentally altering the characters of the resulting compound, was completely at variance with the canons of that theory. But facts remain, while theories must be left either to be adapted to the new state of knowledge, or to be abandoned altogether. In this case the theory has been modified, but even to the present day the interchange of negative chlorine and positive hydrogen is a phenomenon which still affords room for speculation.

One important consequence of the establishment

of the facts of substitution was the inception of the idea of types, a theory which, as remarked by Williamson many years later, was "the vehicle of many an important discovery," and led to profound changes in the way of regarding chemical combination. A most instructive review of the whole position was given by Dumas himself in 1840.[1] He then stated clearly that compounds which contain the same number of equivalents united in the same manner, and which exhibit the same fundamental chemical properties, belong to the *same chemical type.*

This view, though opposed by Berzelius, and at first by Liebig, was afterwards supported by the latter, who cited as analogous the case of chlorine and manganese, which were known in perchlorates and permanganates to be capable of replacing each other without altering the crystalline form of the salt, adding that "a reciprocal substitution of simple or compound bodies, acting in the same way as isomorphous bodies, must be regarded as a veritable law of nature."

Dumas' theory of types, then, expressly recognised the idea of *arrangement* among the constituent particles united together in a compound, and he saw, and stated clearly, the distinction between the older Berzelian system, which attributed to the *nature* of the elements concerned the principal share in deter-

[1] "Mémoire sur la loi des substitutions et la théorie des types" (*Compt. Rend.*, x. 149).

mining the nature of the compound, and the newer doctrine, according to which the number and arrangement of the atoms (or equivalents, as he called them) played the most important part. Dumas, however, does not seem to have perceived so clearly that chemical combination in organic compounds, that is, in compounds of carbon, is governed by the same laws as inorganic compounds; and save for the use which he made of the analogy derived from isomorphism, he did not bridge over the gulf which then separated organic from inorganic chemistry. Hence, while he spoke of alcohol, aldehyd, acetic acid as representing different types, these were not referred by him to substances of a simpler constitution, such as were afterwards employed in the famous system of Gerhardt.

The word "radical" or "radicle" has long held a place in the language of chemistry, but very different meanings have at different times been attached to it. Dismissing as unimportant the use which was made of this word by Lavoisier, and afterwards by Berzelius, we must not omit to recall the fact that in 1832 it received a very definite application in consequence of the discoveries of Liebig and Wöhler. In that year[1] the two great German chemists showed that bitter almond oil, benzoic acid, and many substances derived from them, might all be represented as compounds

---

[1] "Untersuchungen über das Radical der Benzoesäure" (*Liebig's Annalen*, iii. 249).

of one and the same radicle, benzoyl, $C_{14}H_5O_2$ ($C=6$, $O=8$), thus:—

 Hydride of benzoyl . . . . $C_{14}H_5O_2H$
  (bitter almond oil).
 Oxide of benzoyl . . . . $C_{14}H_5O_2O$
  (anhydrous benzoic acid).
 Hydrated oxide of benzoyl . . . $C_{14}H_5O_2O$, HO
  (benzoic acid).
 Chloride of benzoyl . . . . $C_{14}H_5O_2Cl$
 Hydrate of benzoyl . . . . $C_{14}H_5O$, HO
  (benzoic alcohol).

Henceforward it became the object of many chemical investigations to separate and isolate compounds of this kind, which seemed to play the part of elements, and the recognition of which served as the basis for the definition by Liebig of organic chemistry as the *chemistry of compound radicles*, while inorganic chemistry was the chemistry of elementary or simple bodies. One of the most notable discoveries resulting from such investigations was the discovery of ethyl by Frankland in 1848. This substance was obtained by the action of zinc upon ethyl iodide, from which compound it was originally supposed that the metal simply withdrew the iodine, setting the ethyl free. The gas thus obtained was for some years supposed to be the true radicle of ether and alcohol, which were respectively considered to be its oxide and hydrated oxide:—

  Ethyl . . . C_4H_5 ($C=6$)
  Ether . . . C_4H_5O ($O=8$)
  Alcohol . . . C_4H_5OHO

It turned out, however, that this compound really contains in the molecule double these proportions of carbon and hydrogen, and is therefore more correctly expressed by the formula $C_4H_5.C_4H_5$, or C_8H_{10}. ($C = 6$, $O = 8$).

A corresponding revision awaited many others of the isolable radicles, so soon as the law of Avogadro came to be applied, as it was by Gerhardt, to the adjustment of molecular weights. Cyanogen, for example, was not simply C_2N, but $(C_2N)_2$. Kakodyl, in like manner, discovered by Bunsen in 1839, affords another example of a well-defined radicle, which, by union with oxygen, sulphur, and the halogens, affords a long series of compounds. At first, and for many years, represented as $(C_2H_3)_2As$, that is, as arsenious methide, containing two equivalents of methyl, it was afterwards proved to have double that molecular weight.

Gradually, then, it began to be recognised that a "radical" was nothing more than a group of symbols which represented a constituent common to a series of compounds, but not necessarily capable of existence in the free or isolated state. In place of "radical" Gerhardt introduced the word *residue*, defining its application to those portions of a compound which can be transferred to another compound by the process of double decomposition or exchange, and which are not necessarily capable of being isolated. Accordingly, H, Cl, or HO_2 would be entitled to rank as a radical or residue equally with groups such as benzoyl, $C_4H_5O_2$.

The classification of known carbon compounds, which in a few years had become very numerous, was now a matter of urgent necessity. A system based upon the recognition of radicles like methyl, ethyl, benzoyl, &c., had been attempted by Liebig, but without full success, partly because the relations of many of the newly discovered compounds were obscure, and partly because each series was independent and isolated from all others.

The existence of a relation among the successive members of the series of alcohols was first pointed out by Schiel in 1842, and a corresponding relation having been detected by Dumas among the fatty acids, Gerhardt called them "homologous" series. Such a series includes compounds of the same chemical character, the successive terms of which increase by an addition of C_2H_2 ($C = 6$) or CH_2 ($C = 12$), this addition being attended by corresponding rise in the density, boiling point, and, frequently, in the melting points. The arrangement of carbon compounds in homologous series is one which has stood the test of time, but at the period now referred to few such series were known, and these usually imperfectly.

A remarkable effort to bring some system into the chaos then existing was made by Auguste Laurent, whose views were first embodied in a memoir published in 1844,[1] but afterwards in a more elaborate and extended form in a volume

[1] "Classification Chimique" (*Compt. Rend.*, xix. 1089).

which appeared in English only after his death.[1] In this system Laurent supposed every organic compound to contain a *nucleus* composed usually of carbon and hydrogen, and from this fundamental nucleus derived nuclei could be formed by substitution. Thus upon the nucleus, C_4H_4, called etherene, acetic acid, $C_4H_4 + O_4$, was formed, and from the derived nucleus chloretherene, $C_4(H_3Cl)$, chloracetic acid, $C_4H_3Cl + O_4$, was formed. Laurent represented all organic compounds as containing an even number of atoms, and hence was led to employ for many compounds formulæ which were the double of those commonly received. The nucleus theory, though in reality a sort of extension of the theory of radicles, was practically of little use, and was adopted as the basis of classification of organic compounds only in one notable book, namely, in Gmelin's well-known and comprehensive "Handbook of Organic Chemistry." The writings of Laurent, however, must have had a great influence upon the chemical thought of his day, and even now there are pages in his "Chemical Method" which afford refreshing and instructive reading.

But though the theory of *nuclei* did not provide the system of classification so urgently needed, especially for organic compounds, it happened fortunately for the progress of science that the young Laurent became associated with a still younger col-

---

[1] Translated by Odling, 1855 (*Publications of the Cavendish Society*), under the title "Chemical Method."

league, Charles Gerhardt, who joined him in opposition to the dualistic system of Berzelius. Gerhardt's scientific career may be said to have begun when in 1842, at the age of about twenty-six, he published an important series of papers on the classification of organic substances.[1] Here he examined the foundation of the system of equivalents then in use, and showed how a great simplification might be effected, while reducing the whole system of formulæ to a common standard, as already explained (Chap. III.). Laurent finally adopted Gerhardt's system of formulæ, and made use of it in his "Chemical Method." According to this system the formula of each substance represents that quantity of it which, in the state of vapour, would occupy two volumes, the unit volume being the space occupied by one part by weight of hydrogen gas at standard temperature and pressure. Hence, the formulæ of the compounds HCl, H_2O, NH_3, CO_2, C_2H_6O, &c., represent two volumes, while to express the same bulk of the elements and radicles H, Cl, C_2H_5, CN, &c., these atomic symbols must be doubled, thus—

HH or H_2, ClCl or Cl_2, $C_2H_5C_2H_5$ or $(C_2H_5)_2$, CNCN or $(CN)_2$.

The problem involved in the classification of organic compounds was not, however, yet solved. It required a better knowledge of the relations and properties of many compounds, which was only to

[1] "Ueber die Chemische Classification der Organischen Substanzen" (Erdmann's *Jour. f. Prakt. Chemie*, 1842–43).

be obtained by further experimental investigations. To these Laurent and Gerhardt both contributed their full share: Laurent more especially by his work on the hydrocarbon naphthalene, and the numerous derivatives formed from it and from other compounds by the action of chlorine; Gerhardt by his discovery, though much later, of secondary and tertiary amides, and of the anhydrides of acetic and other acids.

The next important step appears to have been taken when in 1849 Wurtz,[1] in studying the action of potash on cyanic and cyanuric ethers, was led to the discovery of the compound ammonias.

Many vegetable matters which possess strong physiological properties have long been known to owe their activity to the presence of definite crystalline or volatile liquid substances, which have the property, in common with ammonia, of combining with acids to form salts. Thus opium contains morphine and other similar compounds, nux-vomica contains strychnine, cinchona bark quinine, while tobacco yields nicotine. In consequence of this basic property these active substances were long ago called alkaloids. So far back as 1837, Berzelius, applying to these substances his own views concerning chemical constitution, expressed the opinion that they consisted of ammonia, which gave them

---

[1] "Sur une Série d'alcalis organiques homologues avec l'ammonique" (*Compt. Rend.*, xxviii. 223, 1849); "Récherches sur les ammoniaques composés" (*Compt. Rend.*, xxix. 169, 1849).

their basic character, united with a "conjunct" composed of carbon with hydrogen or oxygen, by which the character of the ammonia was modified. On the other hand, Liebig in 1840 had expressed the view that if "we were able to replace by amidogen the oxygen in the oxides of methyl and ethyl, in the oxides of two basic radicles, we should, without the slightest doubt, obtain a series of compounds exhibiting a deportment similar in every respect to that of ammonia. Expressed in symbols, a compound of the formula $C_4H_5H_2N = EAd$ would be endowed with basic properties."

Wurtz regarded ammonia as a link between inorganic and organic chemistry, and suggested that if it contained carbon it would be considered as the simplest representative of the organic bases. In his newly discovered bases, C_2H_5N, and C_4H_7N ($C = 6$), he saw organic compounds which might be viewed according to the hypotheses just explained, either as methyl ether, C_2H_3O, or common ether, C_4H_5O, in which 1 equivalent of oxygen was replaced by 1 equivalent of amidogen, NH_2, or as ammonia, in which 1 equivalent of hydrogen is replaced by methyl, C_2H_3, or ethyl C_4H_5.

The following formulæ show these relations :—

H_3N Ammonia, or NH_2H Hydramide.
C_2H_5N Methyl ammonia, or $NH_2C_2H_3$ Methlyamide.
C_4H_7N Ethyl ammonia, or $NH_2C_4H_5$ Ethylamide.

He adds, "Je me servirai de préférence des mots

methylamide, ethylamide," but in the second paper he at once uses, without preface or explanation, the terms *methylamine, ethylamine, valeramine,* to which we have been so long accustomed.

Here, then, it is evident that the great question of chemical "constitution" was beginning seriously to occupy the attention of chemists. Indeed, there is proof that this problem must have arisen already, for the theory of compound radicles introduced by Liebig and Wöhler in 1832, and publicly promulgated by Dumas in 1837,[1] and the still earlier *ammonium* theory of Berzelius, all implied, if they did not explicitly declare, that distinct functions were performed by the different elements composing a given compound. In a paper[2] of Hofmann's a year before Wurtz's discovery, the following passage occurs in reference to the constitution of alkaloids: "A relation between the nitrogen and the saturating capacity remained extremely probable, and chemists now commenced to assume the nitrogen as existing in these bases under two forms. In almost all cases that portion of this element to which the basic properties were referred was believed to be in the form of amidogen, ammonia, or oxide of ammonium, while the views respecting the other portions were for the most part less decided."

Later on, in his memoir on the action of cyanogen chloride, bromide, and iodide on aniline, he expressed

---

[1] *Compt. Rend.,* v. 567; *Brit. Ass. Rep.*
[2] *Jour. Chem. Soc.,* i. 172 (1848).

the view that it is "exceedingly probable that the organic bases are indeed conjugated ammonia compounds." This view, however, he soon modified, for almost immediately afterwards, in discussing the results of experiments made with the object of withdrawing the elements of water from oxalate of aniline, and so obtaining a nitril corresponding to cyanogen, he remarks that "the impossibility of obtaining an anilo-cyanogen throws some doubt on the pre-existence of ammonia in aniline. It is probably more in conformity with truth to consider aniline as a substitution product, as ammonia, in which part of the hydrogen is replaced by phenyl." The ethyl and methyl derivatives of aniline were then produced by the action of ethyl and methyl bromides on aniline,[1] and shown to have the relation to aniline which has ever since been recognised, and which is displayed in the following formulæ :—

$$\text{Aniline.} \quad \left. \begin{array}{l} C_{12}H_5 \\ H \\ H \end{array} \right\} N \qquad \text{Ethylaniline.} \quad \left. \begin{array}{l} C_{12}H_5 \\ C_4H_5 \\ H \end{array} \right\} N \qquad \text{Diethylaniline.} \quad \left. \begin{array}{l} C_{12}H_5 \\ C_4H_5 \\ C_4H_5 \end{array} \right\} N$$

Here, then, was a definite recognition of ammonia as a *type*, upon which was modelled, not only the new artificial compound ammonias, ethylamine, methylamine, and the rest, but all nitrogen compounds possessing basic properties. The acknowledgment of the type ammonia was followed very soon by a corresponding scheme for bringing into

[1] *Compt. Rend.*, xxix. 184 (1849).

one class the numerous and very various compounds known as salts, together with a number of other substances containing oxygen. This conception we owe to Williamson. In 1851 he wrote as follows: "I believe that throughout inorganic chemistry, and for the best known organic compounds, one single type will be sufficient—it is that of water, represented as containing two atoms of hydrogen to one of oxygen, thus—$\genfrac{}{}{0pt}{}{H}{H}O$."[1] In the course of this paper he gave the following formulæ:—

Potash	$\genfrac{}{}{0pt}{}{H}{K}O$
Oxide of potassium	$\genfrac{}{}{0pt}{}{K}{K}O$
Methyl alcohol	$\genfrac{}{}{0pt}{}{H}{CH_3}O$
Ethyl alcohol	$\genfrac{}{}{0pt}{}{H}{C_2H_5}O$
Potassium acetate	$\genfrac{}{}{0pt}{}{C_2H_3O}{K}O$
Anhydrous acetic acid	$\genfrac{}{}{0pt}{}{C_2H_3O}{C_2H_3O}O$
Nitrate of potash	$\genfrac{}{}{0pt}{}{(NO_2)}{K}O$
Hydric chlorite	$\genfrac{}{}{0pt}{}{ClO}{H}O$
Hydric chlorate	$\genfrac{}{}{0pt}{}{ClO_2}{H}O$
Hydric perchlorate	$\genfrac{}{}{0pt}{}{ClO_3}{H}O$

In many cases, however, a multiple of this formula, $\genfrac{}{}{0pt}{}{H}{H}O$, must be used, as in expressing the com-

---

[1] "Constitution of Salts" (*Chem. Gaz.*, 1851, and *Jour. Chem. Soc.*, iv, 1852, 350).

position of bibasic acids and salts like carbonates, sulphates, oxalates. He then explained the action of potash on cyanic ether discovered by Wurtz, and expressed the change by the following diagram:—

$$\begin{array}{cc} K_2 & K_2 \\ O_2 & O_2 \\ (H_2) & (CO) \\ C_2H_5 \quad = \quad C_2H_5 \\ CO & (H_2) \\ N & N \end{array}$$

"One atom of carbonic oxide is here equivalent to two atoms of hydrogen, and, by replacing them, holds together the two atoms of hydrate in which they were contained, thus necessarily forming a bibasic compound $\substack{CO \\ K_2}O_2$, carbonate of potash." This passage is especially noteworthy, for, if not the very first, it is one of the earliest definite expressions of the idea of linkage; that is, of two portions of the same molecule being held together by the agency of an atom or group of atoms which serves as a link between them.

Not long afterwards Williamson also discovered what he called tribasic formic ether, which was obtained by heating together chloroform and sodium ethylate.

$$\begin{array}{c} Cl \\ CH\ Cl \\ Cl \end{array} + \begin{array}{c} NaOC_2H_5 \\ NaOC_2H_5 \\ NaOC_2H_5 \end{array} = CH \left\{ \begin{array}{c} OC_2H_5 \\ OC_2H_5 \\ OC_2H_5 \end{array} \right. + 3NaCl$$

Here manifestly the residue, CH, of chloroform links together three residues of alcohol, OC_2H_5, and combines them in one molecule. It is true that about 1839 Gerhardt had introduced the use of the term "copulated" or "conjugated" as applied to certain compounds, such as the product of the action of sulphuric acid upon benzene or upon benzoic acid, in which sulphuric acid cannot be recognised by the usual tests, and was therefore supposed to be in a state of more intimate union than is found in the sulphates. Berzelius also adopted the same expression, but with a somewhat different meaning, for he seems to have applied the term "copula" to neutral or passive substances supposed to be associated with an active body. Thus acetic acid was regarded by Berzelius as owing its acid properties and chemical activity to oxalic acid, but united with the copula methyl. Evidently these ideas are entirely different, and the *copula* of Berzelius did not connote, as the word might seem to imply, the idea of *holding together* two things which would otherwise separate.

The idea of classifying according to types, then, belongs to Dumas; but for the extension of the idea and modifications by which it was converted into the really serviceable system which it continued to be for many years, it needed the co-operation of many active minds. We have seen how Williamson introduced the water type, and how the discoveries of Wurtz and of Hofmann led to the establishment of the ammonia type. A large number of compounds remained, however, which these two substances, water and ammonia, scarcely seemed to represent. Gerhardt therefore added the hydrochloric acid type and the hydrogen type, and in the fourth volume of his celebrated *Traité de Chimie Organique* he supplied a tabular scheme, showing at a glance how these four types might be made the basis for a system of classification.

To these, as more appropriate to the compounds of carbon, Kolbe added the carbonic acid type; but he used the double value, 12, for carbon, while he retained the equivalent value, 8, for the symbol of oxygen. Hence the formula, CO_4, which he used for the type, represented the oxygen as divisible into four equal parts, whereas there is no reason for believing it to be divisible into more than two parts. The marsh gas type, CH_4, introduced a little later by Kekulé, was of far greater importance.

Further, in 1854 Williamson showed that by the action of phosphorus pentachloride on sulphuric acid a compound is formed, which may be regarded as formed on the conjoint or *mixed* type of hydrochloric acid and water by the introduction of the residue SO_2 in place of two atoms of hydrogen, one derived from each of these compounds, thus:—

$$\left.\begin{matrix}Cl\\H\end{matrix}\right\} \quad \left.\begin{matrix}H\\H\end{matrix}\right\}O \qquad \left.\begin{matrix}Cl\\SO_2\end{matrix}\right\} \quad \left.\begin{matrix}\\H\end{matrix}\right\}O$$

This chlorhydrin of sulphuric acid, or chlorhydrated sulphuric acid, evidently owes its existence to the property possessed by the SO_2 of binding together the Cl and the HO, thus retaining the properties of a chloride joined to those of a hydrate.

In like manner sulphuric acid itself contains the radicle SO_2, which in this compound holds together the residues of two molecules of water. Hence, to represent it, a *condensed* type must be assumed in which two molecules of water are concerned, thus :—

$$\text{Type} \quad \left.\begin{matrix}H\\H\end{matrix}\right\}O \qquad \text{Sulphuric Acid} \quad \left.\begin{matrix}H\\SO_2\\H\end{matrix}\right\}O$$
$$\left.\begin{matrix}H\\H\end{matrix}\right\}O$$

A similar condensed type must be used to represent such acids as phosphoric and arsenic acids,[1] and compounds such as glycol[2] and glycerin,[3] which are not acids but are alcoholic in character.

---

[1] Graham in 1833 first demonstrated the true nature of arsenic and phosphoric acids, and so laid the foundation of the idea of the "basicity" of acids. The following formulæ show the composition of the phosphoric acids, according to the binary system, using equivalents, and for comparison the unitary formulæ, using atomic weights :—

Orthophosphoric acid	. . .	$PO_5 3HO$	H_3PO_4
Pyrophosphoric acid	. . .	$PO_5 2HO$	$H_4P_2O_7$
Metaphosphoric acid	. . .	$PO_5 HO$	HPO_3

See *Alembic Club Reprints*, No. 10.

[2] Glycol was discovered by Wurtz in 1856, as a result of the application of the theory of condensed types to a consideration of the case of glycerin.—" Sur le Glycol ou alcool diatomique " (*Compt. Rend.*, xliii. 199).

[3] "Berthelot was the first to demonstrate the true nature of glycerin as an alcoholic body capable of interacting with three molecules of such acids as acetic and palmitic."—*Ann. Chim.*, xli. 266 (1854).

Triple Water Type.	Phosphoric Acid.	Glycerin.
$\left.\begin{array}{l}H\\H\end{array}\right\}O$	$\left.\begin{array}{l}H\\ \end{array}\right\}O$	$\left.\begin{array}{l}H\\ \end{array}\right\}O$
$\left.\begin{array}{l}H\\H\end{array}\right\}O$	$(PO)\left.\begin{array}{l}H\\H\end{array}\right\}O$	$(C_3H_5)\left.\begin{array}{l}H\\H\end{array}\right\}O$
$\left.\begin{array}{l}H\\H\end{array}\right\}O$	$\left.\begin{array}{l}H\\ \end{array}\right\}O$	$\left.\begin{array}{l}H\\ \end{array}\right\}O$

In such compounds as these three residues of water are linked together in one molecule by the polyatomic radicle.

But while adopting the idea, Gerhardt imposed a strict limitation upon the signification of the word type, as used in his system. For, while the hypothesis of Dumas implied that compounds grouped together were composed of elements arranged in a similar order within the molecule, Gerhardt insisted that any knowledge of what we should now call "constitution" was inaccessible to experiment. The four bodies selected by him as types, namely water, hydrogen chloride, ammonia, and hydrogen, in equal volumes in the state of gas, that is, H_2O, HCl, H_3N, and H_2, he called types of *double decomposition*.[1] Water, for example, in a great variety of transformations, can exchange its hydrogen or oxygen for other elements, giving rise to all the innumerable oxides or sulphides appearing as bases, acids, salts, alcohols, and so forth.

It is difficult for us now to understand why Gerhardt insisted so strongly upon the distinction which he thought he saw between the significance

[1] *Traité de Chim. Org.*, tome iv. 286.

of his own type formulæ and those of Dumas. For when substitution occurs it must be assumed, according to either system, that the radicle which is introduced, whether elementary or compound, takes the same place as the hydrogen or other element which is removed. So that, although it might be asserted that nothing was known, for example, of the arrangement of the atoms in a molecule of water, whatever that arrangement might be assumed to be, it would be maintained in the molecules of all the substances which are fairly to be regarded as derivatives of water.

In the meantime, however, facts were being accumulated in other directions, which subsequently served a most important purpose in the development of the ideas of more modern times in reference to constitution. As already mentioned, Frankland discovered in 1848 the compound which was regarded by all chemists of that time as the free radicle ethyl. In the course of the investigation it was discovered that the zinc does not only combine with the iodine, setting the ethyl free, but that it also combines with a portion of ethyl, producing a definite compound possessed of very remarkable properties. Zinc ethyl, or zinc ethide, ZnC_4H_5, or in modern symbols, $Zn(C_2H_5)_2$, was the first of a long series of "organo-metallic" compounds, the majority of which were prepared and examined by Frankland himself. Writing on the subject many years later, he says:[1] " I had not proceeded far in the

[1] "Experimental Researches" (collected 1877), p. 145.

investigation of these compounds, before the facts brought to light began to impress upon me the existence of a fixity in the maximum combining value or capacity of saturation in the metallic elements which had not before been suspected. That stannous ethide refused to combine with more than the complementary number of atoms of chlorine, &c., necessary to form a molecule symmetrical with stannic chloride, surprised me greatly at first; but such behaviour in this and other organo-metallic bodies scarcely permitted of misinterpretation. It was evident that the atoms of zinc, tin, arsenic, antimony, &c., had only room, so to speak, for the attachment of a fixed and definite number of the atoms of other elements; or, as I should now express it, of the bonds of other elements. This hypothesis constitutes the basis of what has since been called the doctrine of atomicity or equivalence of elements, and it was, so far as I am aware, the first announcement of that doctrine." This statement is justified by reference to the original paper [1] (dated May 10, 1852), in which occurs a clear expression of the view, that in the several compounds of a given element, "*no matter what the character of the uniting atoms may be, the combining power of the attracting element*, if I may be allowed the term, is always satisfied by the same number of these atoms." In other words, the combining capacity of an element does not depend upon the nature of the atoms with

[1] *Phil. Trans.*, cxlii. 417.

which it is united, but is determined by the special character of the element itself.

It appears, then, that while the distinction between univalent and polyvalent atoms and groups of atoms was first perceived by Williamson, we owe to Frankland the first enunciation of the doctrine that each atom possesses a capacity for combination peculiar to itself, and usually limited according to a definite rule.

At this time and henceforward for some years chemists were much occupied with the business of ranging compounds, old as well as new, under their appropriate types, with the natural result that much wrangling ensued upon questions which, when answered, seemed to lose their importance. To what type, for example, should such a compound as nitrous oxide be referred—to the water type or to the ammonia type? Or, again, should chloroform be regarded as a derivative of condensed hydrochloric acid, seeing that in its want of reactivity with silver salts it gave no sign of being a chloride? Gradually it became obvious to all, that the system of types was a merely artificial scheme of classification, as Gerhardt himself had pointed out long ago: "Comme je l'ai souvent dit, mes radicaux et mes types ne sont que des symboles, destinés à concréter en quelque sorte certains rapports de composition et de transformation."[1]

But though types of themselves could serve only

[1] *Traité*, tome iv. 611.

a temporary purpose, and afford merely one point of view, the ideas which arose out of their employment were of the utmost importance; for, as we have seen, they led to the notion of atomic combining power, or "atomicity," and from this sprang the doctrine of the linkage of atoms and modern views as to chemical structure. For this immense stride in advance the world is indebted chiefly to the writings of Kekulé. The question whether the credit of initiating the idea of atomicity belongs to this chemist need not now be discussed, notwithstanding the claim which he put forward some years later,[1] inasmuch as it has already been shown that the idea was first conceived and expressed by Frankland in 1852.[2] Kekulé, however, deserves to be regarded as the founder of modern structural chemistry, inasmuch as the linkage of carbon to carbon is first clearly set forth in his paper "On the Constitution and Metamorphoses of Chemical Compounds, and on the Chemical Nature of Carbon," published in 1858.[3] In this paper he pointed out that the disposition of the atoms constituting a radicle can be represented after sufficient study of its reactions, and in the case of carbon by a study of the compounds of that element. If we consider the simplest compounds of carbon, CH_4, CH_3Cl, CCl_4, $CHCl_3$, CO_2, $COCl_2$, CS_2,

---

[1] "Sur l'atomicité des éléments" (*Compt. Rend.*, lviii. 510, 1864).

[2] This point has been very carefully discussed by Professor Japp in the "Kekulé Memorial Lecture" (*Jour. Chem. Soc.*, lxxiii. 108–120, 1898).

[3] Liebig's *Annalen*, cvi. 129.

CNH, &c., it is obvious, he says, that "the sum of the chemical units which are combined with one atom of carbon is equal to 4. . . . In the case of substances which contain several atoms of carbon, it must be assumed that some of the atoms at least are held in the compound in the same way by the affinity of the carbon, and that the carbon atoms themselves are united together, whereby, of course, a part of the affinity of one is combined with an equal part of the affinity of another. The simplest, and therefore the most probable case of such a union of two carbon atoms, is that in which one unit of affinity of one atom is combined with one unit of the other. Of the 2 × 4 units of affinity of the two carbon atoms, two are employed in holding the two atoms together; there remain, therefore, six which may be united with atoms of other elements. In other words, a group of two atoms of carbon, C_2, is hexatomic; it may form a compound with six atoms of a monatomic element, or generally with so many atoms that the sum of the chemical units of these is six. (Examples: C_2H_6, C_2H_5Cl, $C_2H_4Cl_2$, C_2Cl_6, C_2H_3N, C_2N_2, C_2H_4O, C_2H_3OCl, $C_2H_2O_2$, &c.)

"If more than two carbon atoms unite in the same way, the basicity of the carbon group is increased by two units for each additional atom. The number of atoms of hydrogen (chemical units) which are united in this way with n atoms of carbon, may be expressed as follows:—

$$n(4-2)+2=2n+2.$$

Suppose $n = 5$, the basicity is therefore 12. (Examples: C_5H_{12}, $C_5H_{11}Cl$, $C_5H_{10}Cl_2$, C_5H_9N, &c.) So far it has been assumed that all the atoms associated with the carbon are held by the affinity of the carbon. It may just as well be conceived, that in the case of polyatomic elements, O, N, &c., only a part of the affinity of these, only one of the two units of the oxygen, for example, or only one of the three units of the nitrogen, is combined with the carbon; so that one of the units of affinity of the oxygen, or two out of the three units of affinity of the nitrogen, remain over, and may be united with other elements. These other elements are thus only indirectly combined with the carbon, as indicated by the typical manner of writing the formulæ—

$$\left.\begin{matrix}C_2H_5\\H\end{matrix}\right\}O \quad \left.\begin{matrix}C_2H_5\\H\\H\end{matrix}\right\}N \quad \left.\begin{matrix}C_2H_3O\\C_2H_5\end{matrix}\right\}O \quad \left.\begin{matrix}C_2H_5\\C_2H_5\\C_2H_5\end{matrix}\right\}N$$

Similarly, by means of the oxygen or the nitrogen, different carbon groups are held together."

Further on he refers to the fact that while in a very large number of organic compounds such simple combination of the carbon atoms may be assumed, others exist which contain so much carbon in the molecule, that for them a closer combination of the carbon must be supposed; and then he mentions benzol and its derivatives and homologues, as well as naphthalene, as examples of compounds richer in carbon.

Looking at the position of Gerhardt's system of

types of double decomposition about this time, it is clear that the chief advance which had been made resulted from the recognition of polyatomic radicles, and the power they possess of linking together two or more residues or radicles. As to typical formulæ themselves, though so recently introduced, their importance was already diminishing; for "typical formulæ being representations of reactions, it follows that if a substance affords two or more distinct kinds of reactions, either of formation or of decomposition, it may be consistently represented by formulæ deriving from a corresponding number of distinct types."[1] Hence in a rational formula of the highest possible degree of generality, that is, one which would express all the possible reactions of a body, the constituent radicles must be reduced to the greatest possible simplicity—they must, in fact, be reduced to their elementary atoms. Such a generalised type formula becomes equivalent to a modern constitutional formula. Kekulé himself seems for some time to have hesitated to accept the full consequences of his own conclusions, for while in the paper just quoted he definitely proclaimed the tetratomic character of carbon, and showed how the atoms of this element might combine together, he was writing in his famous *Lehrbuch*[2] "that

[1] See *British Association Report* on the "Recent Progress and Present State of Organic Chemistry," by G. C. Foster (*Report* for 1859, p. 1).

[2] *Lehrbuch der Organischen Chemie oder der Chemie der Kohlenstoff-Verbindungen*, i. 157.

rational formulæ are only formulæ representing the reactions and not the constitution of a body; they are nothing more than expressions for the metamorphoses of a body, and a comparison of different bodies, and are in nowise intended as an expression of the constitution, that is of the arrangement, of the atoms in the actual substance." The reasons he goes on to express for this hesitating position are not quite satisfactory.

Almost at the same time, however, another young chemist, A. S. Couper, in a paper which appeared in all the chief chemical journals, put forth independently quite similar views as to the peculiarities of the element carbon, and by using a system of graphic formulæ had even gone a step further. Couper showed, in the course of his paper, that the quantity of carbon represented by C_2 ($C = 6$) is never divided during chemical changes; hence he remarks: "It is only consequent to write, with Gerhardt, C_2 simply as C, it being understood that the equivalent of carbon is 12."[1] In consequence of peculiar views of his own, however, he retains $O = 8$, and hence all his formulæ contain O_2, or O...O in place of O, but otherwise they resemble modern structural formulæ. As Couper's graphic formulæ are the first symbols of the kind, and are so remarkably like those in common use at the present day, they deserve to be kept in remembrance. One example will suffice;

[1] A. S. Couper, "Sur une nouvelle théorie chimique" (*Ann. Chim.*, liii. 469; *Phil. Mag.* [4], xvi. 104).

propyl alcohol, C_3H_8O, he expressed by the following scheme:—

$$C \begin{matrix} \cdots O \cdots OH \\ \cdots H_2 \\ \vdots \\ C \cdots H_2 \\ \vdots \\ C \cdots H_3 \end{matrix}$$

This was in 1858; in the following year Kekulé's *Lehrbuch* appeared, and in a footnote (p. 160) he introduced a system of graphic formulæ, in which the basicity (*i.e.* valency) of each atom is expressed by the size of the symbol in the following manner:—

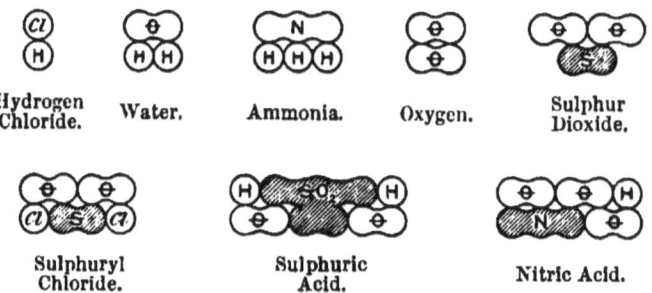

Hydrogen Chloride. Water. Ammonia. Oxygen. Sulphur Dioxide.

Sulphuryl Chloride. Sulphuric Acid. Nitric Acid.

Kekulé thought it necessary to state in a footnote that by these symbols the size of the atoms is not intended, but only the respective number of chemical units of each element. Symbols somewhat similar to these were afterwards used by Naquet and other writers.

Little use of these methods of notation was, however, made for some years, but a system was introduced in 1865 by Professor Crum Brown, which with slight modification has stood its ground and served a valuable purpose. The symbols explain themselves, but the author thought it advisable to state that by them he did "not mean to indicate the physical, but merely the chemical position of the atoms."[1] The formula for ethane, as an example, is on this system as follows:—

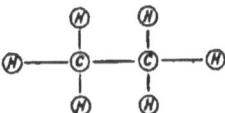

In 1866 Dr. Frankland adopted practically the same system, merely omitting the circles round the symbols of the elements, and henceforward graphic formulæ came freely into general use. By this time the doctrine of atomicity or valency was fully established, and the reluctance which was at first felt by many to use any kind of symbol which seemed to suggest, even remotely, a pictorial representation of a molecule, gradually wore off, in proportion as belief became general in the linking of atoms in definite order as a necessary consequence of the doctrine of atomicity.

From this time forward chemical theory has advanced upon the same road, and mechanical ideas of constitution have more and more permeated the views of chemists as to the mutual relations of

[1] *Jour. Chem. Soc.*, xviii. 232 (1865).

chemically united atoms. This will be developed to some extent in a later chapter, but the subject cannot be relinquished at this point without a brief reference to one important consequence of Kekulé's further study of the question.

The story carries us back to about 1825, when Faraday, in examining the volatile liquid which was wont to collect in the receivers then in use, containing compressed oil gas, discovered *benzol*, or, as it is now written, *benzene*.[1] The same liquid was obtained by Mitscherlich in 1833 as the sole volatile product of the distillation of benzoic acid with lime, the elements of carbon dioxide being abstracted from the acid and retained by the lime in the form of carbonate. Benzoic acid itself was at that time known chiefly as a constituent of a fragrant medicinal resin obtained from a tree, the *Styrax benzoin*, growing in Sumatra. Hence the name of the new compound, which Faraday had analysed and shown to consist of carbon and hydrogen. Coal-tar naphtha was not investigated till about 1847, when Mansfield found in it a more abundant and convenient source of the new hydrocarbon, which henceforward was always manufactured from that liquid. Mitscherlich had discovered that by mixing benzol with strong nitric acid a peculiar aromatic-scented volatile nitro-com-

---

[1] This is not to be confounded with the volatile mixture of liquids known as *benzine* or benzoline, distilled from the lightest parts of petroleum, and which consists of hydrocarbons of the paraffin series, C_nH_{2n+2}.

pound was formed, and this in the hands of the Russian chemist Zinin was converted into the liquid which has long been known as aniline, and which has since become famous as the material from which the earliest of the artificial dyes were produced. Benzol, or benzene, contains carbon and hydrogen in proportions which are most simply represented by the formula CH; but the density of the vapour as compared with that of hydrogen, is such that the molecule must be expressed by six times this formula, or C_6H_6. This compound is the first term of a series of hydrocarbons, of which we owe to the labours of Mansfield the discovery of several members which stand in the relation of homologues to benzene. Thus we have—

Benzene	C_6H_6
Toluene	C_7H_8
Xylene	C_8H_{10}
Cumene	C_9H_{12}
Cymene	$C_{10}H_{14}$, &c.

Some years later Fittig and Tollens proved that all these hydrocarbons can be formed from benzene, by the substitution of methyl CH_3, ethyl C_2H_5, and so forth, for one or more atoms of hydrogen in benzene, and they supplied a method by which this exchange can be actually effected. It soon became obvious that these compounds stood in some very intimate relationship towards essential oil of almonds, essence of cinnamon, essence of cummin, and other fragrant or *aromatic* compounds, among which could be counted hydrocarbons, alcohols, aldehyds, acids, &c. Further, it was recognised that these aromatic compounds presented certain chemical characteristics which distinguish them from the corresponding series derived from fats, and the acids, &c., connected with them. And thus carbon compounds began to be ranged under the two great divisions of *Fatty* and *Aromatic* compounds, which are recognised at the present day. These facts were by 1865 sufficiently established to provide material for reflection, and problems which would have to be encountered by the promoters of the new doctrine of atomic linkage. Kekulé observed that benzene is the first term of the series to which it belongs, and the supposed lower homologue, C_5H_4, was shown to have no existence. The group of six atoms of carbon seems to form a unit which continues to subsist undivided in all the numerous compounds into which the molecule of benzene, more or less stripped of hydrogen, enters as a constituent. Further, the hydrogen in this molecule shows no signs of being gathered round any one or more of the carbon atoms to the disadvantage of the rest. In other words, it is equally distributed among them, so that every atom of carbon has an atom of hydrogen to itself. We have seen how the idea became established, that an atom of carbon is capable of linking itself to a second atom by means of one unit of its atomicity, or valency, as it has been variously called, so that each of the two conjoined atoms loses one-fourth of the power it possesses by itself of becoming attached to other atoms. This may be diagrammatically expressed as follows:—

$$-\overset{|}{\underset{|}{C}}-\overset{|}{\underset{|}{C}}-$$

By the application of the same idea to an indefinite number of atoms, it is easy to conceive of a long chain of carbon atoms linked together in a similar manner, thus:—

$$-\overset{|}{\underset{|}{C}}-\overset{|}{\underset{|}{C}}-\overset{|}{\underset{|}{C}}- \ldots \&c. \ldots -\overset{|}{\underset{|}{C}}-\overset{|}{\underset{|}{C}}-\overset{|}{\underset{|}{C}}-$$

Or again, these atoms may be supposed to be joined in consequence of the suppression of two units of valency between two neighbouring atoms, which may be expressed in a similar manner—

$$=C=C=C=, \&c.$$

Or again, by suppression of one and two units alternately—

$$-\overset{|}{C}=\overset{|}{C}-\overset{|}{C}=\overset{|}{C}-\overset{|}{C}=C\&c.$$

All these are examples of what are now called open chains, in which the terminal atoms have their affinities satisfied by means of hydrogen, chlorine, or some other element which ends the series. The idea which Kekulé introduced is derived very simply from this. He explained the peculiar composition and properties of benzene, by supposing that six atoms of carbon are joined together by alternate single and double linkages, and that *the terminal atoms are united into a closed chain or ring.* This may be expressed by writing the six carbon atoms in a straight line as above, and joining the extremities; but since the molecule of benzene is symmetrical in its chemical behaviour, it has long been the custom to represent it by a symmetrical figure, the hexagon, thus :—

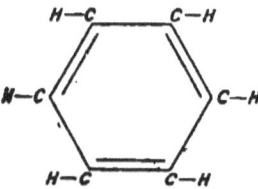

In a large proportion of cases the fourth unit of valency, here, by a guess, represented as linking the carbons together, is simply unaccounted for, and exercised in a way not yet understood; it may, therefore, be left unexpressed. In like manner it is unnecessary to write all the symbols for hydrogen every time the formula is required, and in practice a skeleton symbol has come into use which expresses at once all that is wanted. Further, for reasons which may readily be understood, it is convenient to number the carbon atoms so as to distinguish one from another in the ring, and to signify their relative positions; and so the formula may be reduced to—

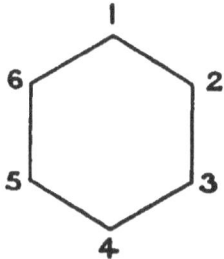

Or more simply as follows, the numbers being understood—

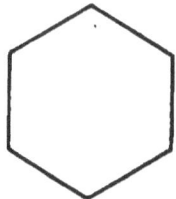

The idea involved in this formula of a chain closed by the interlocking of its terminal atoms has been largely applied, and there is reason now to think that there are groups of compounds formed upon nuclei consisting of 3, 4, and 5, as well as 6 atoms of carbon, and that other elements, such as nitrogen, oxygen, and sulphur, may take a place in the ring. The comparative ease with which rings of six carbons may be formed, and the much greater · difficulty experienced in producing rings made up of three or four atoms of that element, have been explained by hypotheses of a remarkable mechanical character which will be explained in a later chapter. Kekulé's formula, in the simple shape to which it has been reduced by omitting the debatable and much debated question of what becomes of the fourth valency, is accepted by all chemists. Indeed, it may now be regarded as established upon a basis of experimental evidence, comparable with that upon which rests the Atomic Theory itself. It requires in this form no assumptions that have not been fully verified by experiment;[1] and it has rendered such service in the development of " organic " chemistry generally, that it would be no exaggeration to assert, that without it the greater part of modern knowledge in this field could never have been established. Without its guidance a large proportion of the familiar and beautiful artificial colouring matters would probably never have been discovered, and the greater number of the numerous modern synthetical medicinal agents could never have been produced, save, possibly, by accident. The beauty and fertility of Kekulé's theory of the "aromatic" compounds can only be fully appreciated by those who have made a study of the subject,

---

[1] Probably the most important single contribution to the subject ever made is the remarkable memoir by W. Körner, published in 1876, in which he applied the principle, indicated in general terms by Kekulé, by which the problem of the position of radicles introduced by substitution into the molecule of benzene was solved. In working out the application of the method, he described about 120 new compounds. (*Gazzetta Chimica Italiana*, iv., translated and abstracted into the *Journal of the Chemical Society*, 1876, vol. i.)

but the literature relating to this department of chemistry, even for purposes of exposition, is very extensive. It is not possible to enter into more detail in these pages, but the student will readily find in every text-book of "organic" chemistry a statement more or less complete of the applications of the theory.

It has also been well remarked that "Kekulé's structural formulæ cleared away at one stroke the entire brood of pseudo-constitutional formulæ. If organic chemists no longer waste their time in wrangling over the question whether, for example, methylamine is methane, in which one atom of hydrogen is replaced by the amido group, or ammonia, in which one atom of hydrogen is replaced by methyl, the merit is Kekulé's.

"The accuracy of Kekulé's predictions has done more to inspire a belief in the utility of legitimate hypothesis in chemistry, and has, therefore, done more for the deductive side of the science, than that of almost any other investigator. His work stands pre-eminent as an example of the power of ideas."[1]

[1] Professor Japp's "Kekulé Memorial Lecture" (*Trans. Chem. Soc.*, Feb. 1898).

CHAPTER VI

THE DEVELOPMENT OF SYNTHETICAL CHEMISTRY

FROM the time of Lavoisier the subject-matter of chemistry has been divided, in nearly all general treatises on the science, into two chief departments, the mineral or *inorganic*, and the *organic*. In the older text-books vegetable substances were described separately from those of animal origin; but down to comparatively recent times the idea commonly prevailed that the composition and properties of both these classes of compounds were governed by laws differing essentially from those which were found to prevail among substances of mineral nature. It was recognised that organic compounds are usually more complex in composition, and more easily decomposed by heat than minerals, and that " we cannot always proceed, as with materials derived from the mineral kingdom, from a knowledge of their components to the actual formation of the substances themselves. It is not probable," it was said, " that we shall ever attain the power of imitating nature in these operations. For in the functions of a living plant a directing vital principle appears to be concerned peculiar to animated bodies, and superior to and differing from the cause which has been termed chemical affinity" (Henry's "Elements of Experimental Chemistry," 1829). Another purely hypothetical distinction, the result of ignorance of the constitution of the majority of organic compounds, was based upon the assumption of a *binary* plan of combination in inorganic compounds not observable in organic compounds. So late as 1863 the ninth edition of Fownes' "Manual of Chemistry," with Hofmann as joint editor, contains a passage in which it is explained that "copper and oxygen combine to oxide of copper, potassium and oxygen to potassa, sulphur and oxygen to sulphuric acid; sulphuric acid in its turn combines both with oxide of copper and oxide of potassium, generating a pair of salts, which are again capable of uniting to form the double compound $CuO, SO_3 + KO, SO_3$. The most complicated products of inorganic chemistry may be thus shown to be built up by this repeated pairing on the part of their constituents. With organic bodies, however, the case is strikingly different; no such arrangement can be traced."

Organic chemistry then originally, and for a long time, was understood to mean the study of compounds derived from organic sources; but as to the constitution of such compounds, opinion has passed through many successive phases of modification. In 1837 Liebig, in conjunction with Dumas, defined organic chemistry as the chemistry of compound

K

radicles. Gmelin, ten years later, included in the organic division of his "Handbook" compounds which contained more than one atom ($C = 6$) of carbon. Gerhardt's definition is as follows: "La chimie organique s'occupe de l'étude des lois d'après lesquelles se métamorphosent les matières qui constituent les plantes et les animaux; elle a pour but la connaissance des moyens propres à *composer* les substances organiques en dehors de l'économie vivante" (*Traité*, i. 7). But recognising carbon as the essential and characteristic element, Gerhardt made no distinction between those compounds which contain only one atom and those which contain more than one atom of this element. Hence he described as fully the oxides and sulphides of carbon and the carbonates as the more complex compounds which follow in the book.

Kekulé defined organic chemistry as the Chemistry of the Carbon Compounds,[1] and pointed out that the separate treatment of such compounds is chiefly a matter of convenience, and is rendered necessary in consequence of their very large number, and the great practical as well as theoretical importance of so many of them.[2]

---

[1] The title of his well-known treatise expresses this association of ideas: "Lehrbuch der organischen Chemie, oder der Chemie der Kohlenstoff-Verbindungen," 1859.

[2] "Wir definiren also die organische Chemie als die Chemie der Kohlenstoff-Verbindungen. Wir sehen dabei keinen Gegensatz zwischen unorganischen und organischen Verbindungen" (*Lehrbuch*, i. 11).

Kekulé, like Gerhardt, included in his book a description of the oxides and other simple compounds of carbon. Schorlemmer, recognising the important part played by hydrogen in the compounds of carbon, defined Organic Chemistry as the "Chemistry of the Hydrocarbons and their Derivatives." This, however, is a definition belonging to more recent times (*Lehrbuch der Kohlenstoff-Verbindungen oder der Organischen Chemie*, 1872; in English, "A Manual of the Chemistry of the Carbon Compounds or Organic Chemistry," 1874).

The definition of the province of "Organic" Chemistry and investigation of the nature and constitution of "organic" compounds are matters of more than merely technical interest. They concern the great question as to the sources and distribution of energy in nature, and the origin and operation of life itself.

Previously to the publication of Berthelot's *Chimie Organique fondée sur la Synthèse* (1860) no systematic research had been attempted in the direction of building up compounds of carbon, comparable with natural organic compounds, by the union of the elements of which they are composed. Two notable though isolated examples of the production of organic compounds by total synthesis are afforded by Wöhler's formation of urea in 1828, and Kolbe's synthesis of acetic acid in 1845. That Wöhler's discovery should not have attracted more attention than it did for many years is all the more remarkable, because the author himself seems to have been fully aware of its significance. His words are as follows:[1] "J'obtins le resultat inattendu que par le combinaison de l'acide cyanique avec l'ammoniaque il se produit de l'urée; fait d'autant plus remarquable qu'il offre un exemple de la formation artificielle d'une matière organique et même de nature animale au moyen de principes inorganiques. . . . Je ne parlerai pas davantage des propriétés de cette urée artificielle puisqu'elles sont tout-à-fait semblables a celles que l'on peut trouver dans les écrits de Proust, Prout, et autres sur l'urée."

Kolbe's process was more complicated. By the action of chlorine upon carbon bisulphide, which is formed by the union of its two elements, carbon tetrachloride is obtained, and at a red heat this compound is decomposed into chlorine and tetrachlorethylene, C_2Cl_4. In the presence of water, chlorine, and sunlight, this compound yields trichloracetic acid, probably through the intermediate formation of hexchlorethane—

$$C_2Cl_6 + 2H_2O = CCl_3.CO_2H + 3HCl.$$

Trichloracetic acid mixed with water can be reduced to acetic acid by the action of sodium amalgam. It is almost needless to add that the acetic acid prepared by this synthetical process is identical in all respects with the acetic acid obtained from vinegar, which is the product of a peculiar fermentation. It

[1] *Ann. Chim. Phys.* [2], **xxxvii.** 330 (1828).

may be added that Melsens also succeeded, in 1846, in reducing carbon tetrachloride to marsh gas by the action of the same reagents.

The methods employed by Berthelot were for the most part simple and direct. Starting from carbon or one of its oxides, he obtained several hydrocarbons from which, as well known even at that time, more complex compounds can be built up. The following are a few examples of his processes.

At the temperature of the electric arc, carbon and hydrogen unite directly to form acetylene, C_2H_2. The same compound is produced by the action of the electric spark on a mixture of hydrogen with carbonic oxide, with carbon bisulphide, or cyanogen. From acetylene, by acting upon its peculiar copper compound by hydrogen in the nascent state, ethylene is produced. Thus—

$$2xC + xH_2 = xC_2H_2 \text{ acetylene.}$$
$$C_2H_2 + H_2 = C_2H_4 \text{ ethylene.}$$

Ethylene united with the elements of water constitutes common alcohol. To effect this union the gas may be made to combine with a hydracid, especially with hydrogen iodide—

$$C_2H_4 + HI = C_2H_5I,$$

and the resulting compound heated with potassium acetate gives ethyl acetate, from which, by the action of potash, alcohol may be obtained—

$$C_2H_5I + KC_2H_3O_2 = C_2H_5C_2H_3O_2 + KI, \text{ and}$$
$$C_2H_5C_2H_3O_2 + KHO = KC_2H_3O_2 + C_2H_5HO \text{ alcohol.}$$

Alcohol may of course be employed as the starting point for the production not only of aldehyd, acetic acid, or acetone, but of a large number of compounds of more complex composition.

Alcohol, however, is obtainable from ethylene by the simpler process of dissolving the gas in hot sulphuric acid, whereby sulphovinic acid is formed, and subsequently decomposing this compound by distilling it with water.

$$C_2H_4 + H_2SO_4 = C_2H_5HSO_4 \text{ and}$$
$$C_2H_5HSO_4 + H_2O = C_2H_5HO + H_2SO_4.$$

Acetylene may be employed as the material from which benzene and all its multitudinous train of derivatives may be formed, for by the simple application of a moderate heat to the gas it suffers condensation almost completely into benzene—

$$3C_2H_2 = C_6H_6.$$

At higher temperatures more complex hydrocarbons, such as napthalene, $C_{10}H_8$, and anthracene, $C_{14}H_{10}$, are produced. But beside the direct union of carbon with hydrogen at the temperature of the electric arc, the formation of hydrocarbons from these two elements may be accomplished by the addition of one preliminary stage to the series of operations. Thus carbon may be combined with sulphur, forming carbon bisulphide, and hydrogen with sulphur, forming hydrogen sulphide; if, then, these two compounds be transmitted simultaneously through a tube containing heated metallic copper, the sulphur is withdrawn by the metal, and the other elements unite at the moment of their liberation in the presence of each other. A mixture chiefly of marsh gas and ethylene results—

$$2H_2S + CS_2 + 4Cu = 4CuS + CH_4, \&c.$$

Or carbon monoxide may be used as the parent material. This gas is not affected by caustic potash at the common temperature of the air, but at the temperature of 100° and upwards it is absorbed by a concentrated solution of potash with formation of potassium formate—

$$CO + KHO = KCHO_2.$$

From this compound formic acid itself may be obtained, a substance originally procured by the distillation of ants with water, and in more recent times by the oxidation of various materials of vegetable origin.

Such examples as these are sufficient to prove that compounds identical in every respect with the products of animal and vegetable life may be formed from dead mineral matter. Berthelot was so anxious to establish this point beyond the possibility of dispute, that he gives in detail one series of experiments in which the carbon employed was obtained in the form of carbon dioxide from barium carbonate; it was then made to pass successively through the forms of carbonic oxide, formic acid, barium formate, ethylene, ethylene bromide, ethylene again, and finally into ethylsulphuric acid, and its crystallised barium salt from which alcohol, the ultimate object of these experiments, was generated. Water and carbon dioxide, then, were the only compounds from which the elements of this alcohol were derived.

Chemists, then, were long ago completely convinced that so-called "organic" compounds, though frequently more complex than inorganic compounds, such as metallic oxides and salts, owe their existence to the operation of the same chemical affinity which governs the formation and transformation of these compounds. The peculiarities of their constitution arise from the facts pointed out nearly forty years ago by Kekulé and by Couper (see Chapter V.), namely that carbon, the essential element in all such combinations, possesses the remarkable power of *uniting with itself* atom to atom; and secondly, that all the combining units of such an atom or group of atoms *may be saturated by hydrogen.*

Considering the now universal recognition of the true province of Organic Chemistry, it is unfortunate that the names *Inorganic* and *Organic* should be still retained for the two co-ordinate departments of the science, and that the division between them, though practically necessary, should be maintained in so absolute and arbitrary a manner. To speak of *Organic* chemistry at all, is only one of the many examples which might be given of the etymological confusion which everywhere prevails in the language of chemistry. There are organic beings, and there may be a chemistry peculiar to their functions, but this is what would be rightly comprehended under the term physiological chemistry, or rather chemical physiology. All chemists, however, now agree that there is but one chemistry so far as principles are concerned, no matter how various may be its applications. The sharp distinction and separation of inorganic and organic chemistry is in teaching and learning a source of great loss and inconvenience; for until a student has become acquainted with the properties of at least a few carefully selected carbon compounds, he can have no true idea of the relation of composition and constitution to physical properties, which is only to be acquired by the study of the phenomena of isomerism and of series. Among metallic and mineral compounds there is nothing corresponding to homologous series, unless we admit the relations which have been traced (see Chap. IV.) between the atomic weights of certain elements and their properties. But these are far less regular than the relations observable among the members of a series like the acetic series of acids. Moreover, a student who is limited to the study of salts and other metallic compounds has few opportunities of observing the methods by which "constitution" is established, and even the processes and effects of oxidation and reduction can be but imperfectly understood.

Since the time of Berthelot's experimental investigation of the conditions under which such carbon compounds may be formed, the art of chemical synthesis, the building up of complex from simple materials, has made remarkable progress. Not only the simple formic and acetic acids, but complex vegetable acids, such as tartaric, citric, salicylic, gallic, cinnamic; not marsh gas and ethylic alcohol only, but phenols, indigo, alizarin, sugars, and even alkaloids identical with those extracted from the tissues of plants, are now producible by purely chemical processes in the laboratory. It might appear that such triumphs would justify anticipations of still greater advances, by which it might become possible to penetrate into the citadel of life itself. Nevertheless the warning that a limit, though distant yet, is certainly set in this direction to the powers of man, appears to be as justifiable now, and even as necessary, as in the days when all these definite organic compounds were supposed to be producible only through the agency of a "vital force." Never yet has any compound approaching the character and composition of albumen or any proteid been formed by artificial methods, and it is at least improbable that it ever will be without the assistance of living organisms. But even supposing the secret of the chemical constitution of all the colloidal proteid substances fully understood, the eloquent words of Gerhardt are just as true as ever: "Jamais le chimiste ne saura produire dans son laboratoire ni un muscle, ni un nerf, ni une feuille, ni une fleur, ni la plus légère fibre; car à supposer même qu'il apprenne à composer toutes les matières qui constituent les muscles, les nerfs, les feuilles, les fleurs, les fibres végétales, il manquera toujours de la libre disposition de cet agent inconnu qui coordonne ces matières en organes doués de vie, c'est-à-dire doués d'un mouvement propre, différent de celui qu'impriment à la matière les attractions chimiques" (*Traité*, i., Introduction, iv.).

Emphasis has been recently [1] laid upon a physical distinction between living and dead matter, which has for many years been suspected. Notwithstanding the remarkable advances in synthetical chemistry, of which a few salient examples are described in this chapter, one result has never yet been achieved, and that is the production by purely chemical processes, and without the aid of living matter, of a compound possessing the power of rotating the plane of polarisation of a ray of polarised light, in the manner which is so characteristic of many of the proximate constituents of animal and vegetable structures, such as the proteids, the sugars, and various hydrocarbons, acids, and alkaloids. This question will be discussed in the next chapter. It is sufficient to remark here that this distinction is, after all, arbitrary and artificial, and possibly, nay, even probably, will disappear before the light of more knowledge derived from further experimental investigation, just as the "vital force" of the older school was shown, full forty years ago, to be unneces-

[1] See "Address to the Chemical Section of the British Association," Bristol, 1898, by Professor F. R. Japp, President of the Section.

sary to the formation of even the most complicated among definite compounds of carbon.

The methods employed by the modern chemist in the construction of carbon compounds, the molecules of which are known to contain many atoms of carbon, are so numerous that it is not possible in such a sketch as this to do more than indicate broadly their general nature. It has already been shown how Berthelot and others succeeded in uniting the elements carbon, hydrogen, oxygen, and nitrogen into compounds previously believed to be derivable only from organic sources, but such substances as formic acid, alcohol, and acetic acid are after all very simple in constitution, and between such compounds as these and the common constituents of vegetable and animal juices there is a wide interval. Tartaric acid, for example, contains four atoms of carbon, citric acid six atoms, common sugar twelve atoms of the same element, while caffeine, the alkaloid of tea and coffee, contains eight atoms of carbon with four atoms of nitrogen; and the blue colouring matter of indigo contains sixteen atoms of carbon and two atoms of nitrogen in the molecule. The art of uniting carbon to carbon has now become so familiar, that chemists are apt to forget that its discovery and application is so recent that it really belongs to the present generation. Before attempting to illustrate by an example or two the nature of the methods employed, it is necessary to remind the reader that advances in the direction referred to postulate certain fundamental ideas, the origin and development of which has already (Chap. V.) been described. We believe now that in a molecule the constituent atoms are not thrown together confusedly in a general jumble, but that a definite order is maintained, and that this order can be, at least with great probability, inferred from the properties, modes of formation, and decomposition of the compound. In such a system it is recognised that some elements are united together *directly* and some *indirectly*, according to their respective valencies, into a structure which, though it doubtless possesses great elasticity, is more or less permanent. So long as the compound retains its identity its constituent atoms do not wander about, but retain their relative positions; whereas, if a change of relative position does occur, this is immediately manifested by a change in the properties or chemical behaviour of the substance. The knowledge which we now possess of the "constitution" of so large a number of chemical compounds is, of course, the outcome of an immense amount of patient labour, the utility of which has not always been obvious to the unlearned.

One method of uniting carbon to carbon is based upon the peculiar properties of cyanogen and its compound with hydrogen, hydrocyanic or prussic acid. Cyanogen is very familiar as a compound radicle which is capable of playing the same kind of part as chlorine or bromine, and of being exchanged for either of those elements. If, then, such a substance as ethylene, which, as already explained, can be prepared from its elements, is first converted into its bromide, $C_2H_4Br_2$, the bromine may be exchanged for cyanogen by simply heating it with potassium cyanide. The compound ethylene cyanide, $C_2H_4(CN)_2$, results, and if this is boiled with an acid or an alkali the nitrogen is removed in the form of ammonia, while an equivalent quantity of oxygen and hydrogen is introduced, and succinic acid, $C_2H_4(CO_2H)_2$, is obtained. This was accomplished by Maxwell Simpson in 1861, and since the means of converting succinic acid into racemic acid had been previously made known by Perkin and Duppa, here was a method of building up a complex vegetable acid by a process of purely chemical synthesis.

This succession of operations may be traced in the following series of formulæ, which serve to show how the chemical constitution of tartaric acid has been determined :—

$$\begin{matrix} CH_2 \\ \| \\ CH_2 \end{matrix}$$ Ethylene.

$$\begin{matrix} CH_2.CN \\ | \\ CH_2.CN \end{matrix}$$ Ethylene cyanide.

$$\begin{matrix} CH_2.CO.OH \\ | \\ CH_2.CO.OH \end{matrix}$$ Succinic acid.

$$\begin{matrix} CHBr.CO.OH \\ | \\ CHBr.CO.OH \end{matrix}$$ Dibromo-succinic acid.

$$\begin{matrix} CH(OH).CO.OH \\ | \\ CH(OH).CO.OH \end{matrix}$$ Tartaric or racemic acid.

Hydrocyanic acid has the power of uniting with many compounds, especially with aldehyds and ketones, in such a manner that its carbon becomes attached to the carbon of the aldehyd or ketone, while the nitrogen can afterwards be eliminated, if desired, by the action of dilute acids or alkalis, as already explained. In this way, for example, lactic acid, $C_3H_6O_3$, the acid of sour milk, may be formed from aldehyd, C_2H_4O.

Another method of producing more complex from simple carbon compounds is founded on the tendency of many of them to undergo the process of polymerisation, or formation of new molecules by the union of several into one. The polymerisation of acetylene into benzene has been already mentioned, and to this may be added such cases as the conversion of aldehyd into paraldehyd,

$$3C_2H_4O = C_6H_{12}O_3,$$

and the production of the sugar-like substances formose from formaldehyd,

$$6CH_2O = C_6H_{12}O_6,$$

and acrose from glyceric aldehyd,

$$2C_3H_6O = C_6H_{12}O_6.$$

Many of such changes occur spontaneously in course of time or under the influence of heat.

In other cases condensation is effected by the use of agents which have a tendency to unite with water or with ammonia, which may be separated from the elements of the parent substance as a by-product. For example, acetone mixed with strong sulphuric acid yields water and trimethyl-benzene or mesitylene—

$$3C_3H_6O = C_9H_{12} + 3H_2O.$$

Another very interesting method of joining carbon to carbon arises out of the remarkable influence exercised by oxygen upon the properties of hydrogen atoms attached, not to the oxygen itself but to carbon atoms near to it within the molecule. Malonic acid, for example, contains a series of three carbon atoms, of which the central is united with two atoms of hydrogen, while the two lateral are combined with oxygen, thus:—

$$-CO-CH_2-CO-$$

Now, when carbon is united to hydrogen only, the hydrogen is incapable of being disturbed by the action of sodium, and in compounds which contain three carbon atoms thus united, but all combined with hydrogen, contact with sodium or a sodium compound would have no effect. But if the ethereal salt of malonic acid is mixed with sodium ethylate, one of the two atoms of hydrogen is immediately replaced by sodium, thus:—

$$-CO-CHNa-CO-$$

The sodium thus introduced may be easily exchanged for a hydrocarbon radicle — ethyl, for example — by bringing the new compound into contact with the iodide, while the sodium is eliminated in the form of sodium iodide. A compound thus results, in which the carbon of the ethyl is attached to the carbon which was previously provided with hydrogen only,

$$-CO-CH-CO$$
$$|$$
$$C_2H_5$$

The synthetical formation of large numbers of complex compounds has been effected by making use of this principle.

Enough has now been said to indicate the lines upon which research has travelled during the last thirty years or more, but it must be obvious that the practical success of such operations is greatly dependent upon providing the right physical conditions, and these can only be arrived at as the result of much experience in the laboratory.

The artificial production of complex carbon compounds, possessing properties which render them applicable to a great variety of practical purposes, may be justly regarded as one of the triumphs of modern chemistry. Many of these compounds, such, for example, as salicylic acid, used extensively as an antiseptic and as a remedial agent in medicine, indigo and alizarin as dyes, coumarin and vanillin as perfumes, are identical with the compounds previously known only as products of vegetable life, and obtainable only from the substance of the several plants which yield them. Some of these discoveries, in consequence of which it has become possible to dispense with the cultivation or collection of large quantities of a plant, have been followed by economic results of far-reaching effect. One of the most notable instances of this kind is supplied by the case of alizarin, the chief red colouring matter of the madder root. The cultivation of this plant, the *Rubia tinctoria* of the botanist, of which the wild variety is found commonly in hedges in Britain, has been for centuries carried on in the south of Europe. It was introduced into the south of France in 1766 by Jean Althen, to whom a statue was erected at Avignon, in recognition of the value of this service to the district. But in 1868 the relation of alizarin to anthracene, a hydrocarbon present in the less volatile portion of coaltar oil, was established by Graebe and Liebermann. Methods were immediately devised by W. H. Perkin in this country, and by Caro, Graebe, and Liebermann in Germany, by which the manufacture of alizarin from anthracene became commercially possible. Henceforth the cultivation of the madder plant in the countries in which previously it had been a crop of considerable money value, and occupying large tracts of land, became unnecessary, and it therefore speedily declined, and has now almost disappeared. Dr. Perkin states[1] that the value of the imports of madder root into the United Kingdom had been previously about one

---

[1] Lectures before the Society of Arts, 1879.

million pounds sterling per annum; and when we reflect upon this, and upon the influence which is imposed upon the inhabitants of a country district by the necessity of learning new methods of cultivation, and of finding new markets, as the consequence of the exchange upon so large a scale of one kind of crop for others, perhaps untried, the great importance of such a discovery becomes obvious.

Of the very numerous substances now emanating from the chemical laboratory, many others, like alizarin and indigo, are applicable as dyes, either to cotton on the one hand, or to wool and silk on the other. Substances like alizarin require the previous application to the fabric of some substance, called a "mordant," with which they can unite, forming a compound which is not only insoluble in water, and therefore is not washed out by water, but also exhibits a brighter and characteristic colour, the tint of which is determined by the mordant employed. Thus with alizarin a red colour is produced by alumina, a purple by peroxide of iron. The most famous of these artificial substances of strong tinctorial power are, of course, the so-called "aniline dyes," and these for the most part require no mordant when applied to wool and silk. The story of the discovery of the first of these colours, the substance originally called *mauve*, or aniline purple, has become so familiar, and has been followed by so many other wonders, that its interest may be thought to have faded; but to Englishmen it ought always to serve both as a source of justifiable pride and as a warning for the present and the future. This discovery was made and was worked out into a practical process of manufacture in 1856 by our distinguished countryman, Dr. W. H. Perkin, whose name has already been mentioned in connection with alizarin. But the manufacture of the vast series of colouring matters of every shade and tint, of which mauve must be regarded as the ancestor, has been gradually transferred to Germany, where the cultivation of "organic" chemistry has been fostered in the universities and technical high schools, while it has been comparatively neglected in the corresponding institutions of this country.

The history of the development of the coal-tar colour industry would alone be sufficient to occupy several volumes, and it is therefore impossible to do justice to it in these pages;[1] but it should be mentioned that the name "aniline," applied popularly to these colours, is in a great many cases entirely a misnomer. Mauve and magenta were the colours first obtained, and they were formed by the action of oxidising agents upon aniline, or rather upon a mixture of aniline with some of its homologues, especially toluidine. A large proportion of the colours now manufactured are produced by chemical changes from other

[1] An exceedingly interesting account was given by Dr. Perkin of his own career, and of the discovery of mauve and other colours, in connection with the Hofmann Memorial Lecture, May 1893, of which a full report appears in the *Transactions of the Chemical Society* for 1896.

substances obtained from the constituents of coal-tar, for example, naphthalene, and by the application of wholly different methods, of which the most important is the process known as "diazotisation," discovered by P. Griess in 1865. This consists in the introduction of two atoms of nitrogen, combined on the one hand with carbon, and on the other with an acid radicle or other group. Most of these compounds are unstable, and decompose with explosion when heated or struck, and are often rapidly affected by light.

The problem presented by the intense colour and tinctorial power of the "organic" colouring matters has been much debated during the last five-and-twenty years, but so far without the establishment of any general theory. In fact, it seems improbable that substances so diverse in composition and in constitution should agree in any one peculiarity of structure, to which the property of selective absorption of light, that is, of colour, can be fairly attributed. And if, for example, a particular molecular configuration is indeed connected with the production of a red or yellow colour, it seems likely that not the same, but some other configuration would be required to transmit or to absorb vibrations of very different wave-length belonging to the blue or violet order of colours. Many of the facts observed must, however, be admitted to be tempting. For example, the very general development of yellow colour by the introduction of the nitro group NO_2

into compounds, which are themselves colourless. Phenol, C_6H_5OH, is perfectly white, nitric acid and nitrates generally are white; but the product of the interaction of phenol and nitric acid is picric acid, $C_6H_2(NO_2)_3OH$, a common yellow dye. The diazo group is also connected with the production of colour.

The influence of molecular weight in modifying the shade of colour was one of the first observations of this kind made, and it was attended with practical results of great importance. The red dye of aniline,—fuchsine, magenta, or rosaniline,—as it has been variously called, was converted into a series of other dyes, in which the red was gradually suppressed and blue developed, by the introduction of methyl, ethyl, phenyl, and naphthyl groups, which are simply composed of carbon and hydrogen, in place of one or more atoms of hydrogen in the original dye stuff. We thus arrive at the following series:—

$C_{20}H_{21}N_3O$	Red.
$C_{20}H_{18}(CH_3)_3N_3O$	Reddish violet.
$C_{20}H_{18}(C_2H_5)_3N_3O$	Pure violet.
$C_{20}H_{18}(C_6H_5)_3N_3O$	Blue.

A remarkable fact about these compounds is that the bases themselves, of which the formulæ are given above, are colourless, and it is only in the form of salts that they behave as dyes.

Turning from the production of colouring matters, a survey of the applications of "organic" chemistry to useful purposes reveals such a variety and wealth of material that the pages of no single book could contain even a superficial sketch of the whole. And it is not possible, therefore, in this place to do more than point out the most important of the directions in which the greatly enlarged knowledge of these modern times has been applied.

The arts of peace and of war have alike profited by the discoveries of the chemist. In medicine the physician is now provided with a bewildering host of new agents. The introduction of antiseptics by Lister produced a revolution in the practice of surgery as great as that which resulted from the use of the anæsthetics by which pain is abolished, and both these classes of agents are obtained from the laboratory of the chemist. And now we have a choice of a great variety of chemical compounds produced by synthetical processes, and of which the physiological action has been more or less completely investigated and shown to be applicable to the treatment of disease. It is only necessary to recall a few out of the scores of substances which have been proposed for use. Among antipyretics there are antifebrine (acetanilide, $C_6H_5.NH.C_2H_3O$), phenacetine (aceto-para-phenetidine, $C_6H_4(OC_2H_5).NH.C_2H_3O$), and antipyrine or phenazone (phenyl-dimethyl-isopyrazolone,

$$\begin{array}{c} CH - CO \\ \| \quad\quad\quad >N.C_6H_5 \\ C.CH_3 - N.CH_3 \end{array}).$$

Among anodynes and hypnotics there are paraldehyd ($C_6H_{12}O_3$), chloral ($CCl_3.COH$) and its combinations, sulphonal (dimethyl - methane - diethyl sulphone $(CH_3)_2C(SO_2C_2H_5)_2$), and others. Among anæsthetics there are not only the long familiar chloroform and ether, but many substances of value for the production of local insensibility to pain. Of these, the alkaloid cocaine and its various derivatives and substitutes are the most remarkable. The employment of antiseptics has extended beyond the application made by the surgeon in the treatment of wounds, and the sanitarian as disinfectants, to the preservation of milk, meat, fish, and various other articles of food, until it has now become a question whether the use of these substances in an indiscriminate manner may not before long require some legislative restriction.

The use of explosives is not now confined to their applications to warlike purposes. The discovery of nitro-glycerin and its employment in the form of "dynamite" have contributed in no small degree to the assistance of work which makes for peace, in road and tunnel making, in quarrying, in shattering rocky obstructions in rivers, and generally to the purposes of the engineer. Discovered by Pelouze about 1838, gun-cotton has long been a famous explosive; but the difficulties attending its manufacture and storage at first interfered with its production on a large scale, while the rapidity of its explosion, as compared with that of the old black gunpowder, prevented for a long time its use for artillery purposes. By attention to certain details in the purification of the cotton, both before and after its immersion in the nitric acid, the stability of the product is now insured; and by mixing it with other nitrates, and with various combustible, but not explosible, substances which serve to diminish the rapidity of its combustion, and so damp the violence of its action upon the gun, explosives are now freely manufactured which are applicable to sporting as well as to warlike purposes. These mixtures, known under the names of Schultze's powder, cordite, &c., are valued for their smokeless combustion.

It is unnecessary to add further to the list of applications which have been made of the "chemic art" so far as concerns compounds of which the atomic framework is composed of carbon. The development of the industrial production of organic dye-stuffs, drugs, antiseptics, explosives, illuminating oils and gases, perfumes, artificial substitutes for india-rubber, ivory, parchment, and many other things familiar in daily life, proceeds with increasing rapidity, and the pages of journals of chemistry are crowded with the description of new compounds. The fertility of the methods employed seems to show that for the present the commonly accepted views of structural chemistry are sufficient, and will perhaps prevail for some years to come. There are, however, indications that ideas of valency require considerable modification, and when that modification has been agreed upon changes in formulæ will undoubtedly follow.

Some earlier pages of this chapter were occupied with the consideration of the successive discoveries by which it has been shown that many of the definite chemical compounds, which were formerly derived solely from organic sources, have been successively produced by the operations of the chemist, independently of animal and of plant. Any one who attentively considers the details of such laboratory processes as have been described, must at once perceive that the chemist and the organism proceed by very different ways to the attainment of the same result. The methods of the laboratory commonly require the employment of strong chemical agents, caustic alkalis, acids, and the like, as well as a high temperature. The range of temperature within which processes of growth, of secretion, or of excretion go on in the plant or animal is restricted to a few degrees; and the chemical changes occur within a medium, the sap or blood, the composition of which is extremely complicated, and altogether unlike any reagent employed by the chemist. Whether it will ever be possible to discover the precise nature and order of the changes by which a plant, for example, produces sugar or starch out of carbonic acid and water, is a question which does not admit of profitable discussion in the present state of knowledge; but the study of the remarkable changes which go on in the long familiar process of alcoholic fermentation has led to a great extension of our knowledge of one class of agents employed in the living organism, and a brief outline of the successive theories which have been advanced in regard to the nature of the fermentive process itself will not be out of place. As every one knows, wine is made from grape-juice, beer from solution of malt or sugar, cider from the juice of apples, and so forth. It is also familiar knowledge that the beverages which result agree in containing alcohol, which is formed, together with carbonic acid, out of the elements of the sugar originally present in the liquid, and which after fermentation is much reduced, or altogether disappears. But every one does not know what are the conditions which are essential to this transformation, and what products, if any, are formed along with the alcohol and carbonic acid. Thanks to the researches of Pasteur, these conditions are now pretty well established. A solution of pure sugar in water may be kept without change for an indefinite length of time, but if to this liquid is added a minute amount of a phosphate, together with a little nitrogenous matter, even in the inorganic form of an ammonium salt, fermentation will set in almost immediately on addition of a small quantity of yeast, or, after a longer and variable interval of time, if the liquid is exposed freely to the air. If yeast has not been added, it will nevertheless be found in the liquid as soon as fermentation has manifestly commenced, and its presence has been traced to the admission of stray yeast cells or spores, which are now known to exist along with other organisms, in countless numbers, floating in the air. During the process the temperature must not be allowed to fall below about 40° F., nor to rise much above 80° F.

The destruction of the sugar is indicated by the gradual loss of sweetness by the solution, carbon dioxide gas makes its escape with effervescence, and the liquid retains alcohol with a small quantity of glycerin and succinic acid, which are always produced, though the source of them is still a little uncertain. If a definite amount of yeast has been added, it will be found to have increased in quantity, and the cells of which it is composed show under the microscope the process of multiplication by budding.

Reduced to its simplest form, this is the phenomenon exhibited during the change of sweet vegetable juices into wine, an art which has been practised from the earliest times of which tradition brings us an account. Notwithstanding its great antiquity, however, no definite knowledge concerning the nature of the process was secured until times well within the period to which this book refers, and although various theories were propounded at successive periods, from alchemical times onwards, they were for this very reason all beside the mark. The changes which have occurred within the last fifty years in the hypotheses relating to alcoholic fermentation, have been brought about in consequence of the gradual recognition of the essential part played in the process by the yeast which is always present.

Of the several theories in the field forty years ago, the most generally accepted was that of Liebig. Regarding yeast merely as a putrescent mass, he supposed the peculiar state of atomic motion, hypothetically prevailing in all substances in that condition, to be transmitted by contact with the sugar to the atoms of that compound, which were thus shaken asunder so as to give rise to new products more stable than itself. This kinetic idea, not objectionable in itself, but only because it paid no regard to established facts, Liebig maintained in some form or other to the end of his life. But in science fact stands before authority, and notwithstanding the influence of the great German chemist, his theory was on the point of being finally overthrown at the very time when, at the head of one of his celebrated "Letters on Chemistry," he was declaring the "theory which ascribes fermentation to fungi refuted."[1] For in 1857 Pasteur began the long series of researches on fermentation upon which so large a part of his great fame rests. Reviving almost forgotten observations of Cagniard de la Tour and of Schwann, who had established the true nature of yeast as a unicellular organism of spheroidal form, invariably associated with alcoholic fermentation, and the life and fermentive activity of which was destroyed by heat, Pasteur completely established the

[1] Fourth edition, 1859, Letter xxi.

vitalistic theory of the process. According to this doctrine the change of sugar into alcohol and carbonic acid is a consequence of the multiplication in the solution of the cells of the yeast which, for the purposes of its own growth, apparently uses the sugar as its food; while the alcohol and carbonic acid are to be regarded as excretory products, the glycerin and succinic acid being perhaps products of metabolism in the constituents of the organism itself. Here is, then, an example of chemical changes which accompany the development of a specific organism under certain definite conditions. If the organism is changed, or the conditions are changed, different effects ensue.

But the decomposition of sugar into alcohol and carbonic acid is not the only change which may be spoken of as fermentation. The lactic ferment is another organism more minute than yeast, and presenting a different rod-like form, which has the power of changing sugar into lactic acid. In this case the action soon comes to an end if the liquid is allowed to become acid, but this is easily prevented by stirring into the liquid a sufficient quantity of chalk, which neutralises the acid as fast as it is produced. A third organism is endowed with the specific function of breaking up lactic acid into butyric acid, carbon dioxide, and hydrogen. In this case a peculiarity of the process consists in the fact that the presence of air is unfavourable to the development of the organism, and is even capable of suspending the process of fermentation. In like manner it has come to be recognised that a considerable number of changes, formerly supposed to be purely chemical, are brought about by the influence of minute cellular organisms, some of which are known as *bacteria* (βακτηρία, a stick or staff) or *bacilli* (*bacillum*, a little stick), from their cylindrical, rodlike, or spindle-shaped forms.

The vitalistic theory of fermentation connects the chemical changes, of which alike the materials and the products have in many cases long been known, with the existence of certain lowly forms of life. The presence of these organisms in contact with the liquid, under proper conditions, determines the decomposition which in their absence does not take place. This theory was practically established by the researches of Pasteur by the year 1861, and though in some minor particulars further knowledge is very desirable, the recognition of the main principle has been attended with consequences of importance so great as to be inestimable; for by means of these earlier discoveries Pasteur was led to the still more valuable pathological investigations which followed continuously down to the close of his life. To say that Pasteur effectually and finally disposed of the doctrine which affirmed the possibility of spontaneous generation, and that from the organic theory of fermentation he was led to the "germ theory" of disease, is to repeat what is familiar to all the world; but it is not possible in this place to follow the course of the marvellous discoveries connected with the chemical and physiological effects of micro-organisms, or ferments, as they may all be called. And reference is made to this subject only in order to lead back to a series of facts which have gradually come to light concerning the chemical properties and reactions of certain nitrogenous constituents of animal and of vegetable tissues. The compounds referred to are soluble in water, are coagulable, and in any case rendered inert by the application of heat, as well as by contact with strong chemical agents. Such compounds, which doubtless originate in some, at present mysterious, change in the "protoplasm," or living substance, are endowed with the power of transforming a relatively large quantity of some other compound into simpler material. They are generally referred to as *enzymes*, or sometimes less appropriately as soluble ferments. These substances are very widely diffused in both the animal and vegetable kingdoms, and many of them are concerned in processes which have been long familiar. Thus it has been known for a century or more that malt contains a soluble material to which the name *diastase* has been given, which has the power of rendering starch soluble in water by converting it into a kind of sugar. One of the most familiar of enzymes is the substance contained in rennet, a fluid obtained from the stomach of the calf, which has the power of coagulating the casein of milk, and is for this purpose employed extensively in the manufacture of cheese. It has also long been known that sweet and bitter almonds in the dry state are both without special odour, but that when the bitter almond is crushed in the presence of water, the characteristic volatile essence, consisting of benzaldehyd, begins immediately to be formed. It was Liebig who discovered that the bitter almond contains a crystalline substance, amygdalin, $C_{20}H_{27}NO_{11}$, which, in contact with a peculiar soluble albuminous matter existing in both sweet and bitter almonds, is resolved by the assumption of the elements of water into glucose, prussic acid, and benzaldehyd. The pungent oil of mustard is developed in an entirely similar way. In the "pepsin" of the animal stomach there is another example of a soluble enzyme, which in this case is specially active in causing the degradation and simplification of the complex albuminoids of food, converting them into soluble materials called "peptones," which probably pass directly into the blood and are assimilated. Great attention has been given of late years to the recognition of these enzymes, and to the study of the changes which they bring about. Their remarkable activity is still a mystery, but the rapidity and energy of their special effects are often greater than the corresponding effects produced by the recognised chemical agents of the laboratory.

It has been stated that the peculiar function of these compounds is "hydrolytic"; that is, they are believed to act by causing the addition of the elements of water to a great variety of compounds

M

which are then resolved into simpler molecules. This does, indeed, appear to be the usual mode of action exercised by these remarkable and complex substances. Nevertheless there is evidence that in some cases at any rate the process is reversible, in the same sense that so many other chemical changes are reversible, in consequence of the interfering influence of the accumulation of the products of change.

Cane sugar under the influence of an enzyme extracted from yeast yields "invert sugar," a mixture of equal numbers of molecules of glucose and fructose—

$$C_{12}H_{22}O_{11} + H_2O = C_6H_{12}O_6 + C_6H_{12}O_6.$$

Maltose, which is isomeric with cane sugar, splits under similar conditions into two molecules of glucose—

$$C_{12}H_{22}O_{11} + H_2O = 2C_6H_{12}O_6.$$

It has been lately discovered[1] that this process in the case of maltose is hindered by adding glucose to the liquid, and that when the enzyme is added to a strong solution of glucose some of it is converted into maltose. Whether a solution of maltose or a solution of glucose of the same concentration is employed, the tendency is to the production of a state of equilibrium among the products of the change, so that the liquid ultimately contains

[1] A. C. Hill, "Reversible Zymohydrolysis" (*Trans. Chem. Soc* 1898, p. 634).

maltose and glucose in the same proportions to each other.

But some of these soluble enzymes appear to be capable of acting in an altogether different way, for it has been found quite recently (1897) by E. Buchner[1] that yeast cells, when ruptured by grinding with sand and a little water, yield a liquid which, after filtration, has the power of producing the fermentation of sugar, although it appears to be quite free from yeast cells. The soluble substance so obtained is apparently allied to the proteids, and its power is destroyed by heating to about 50° C., whereby an albuminous substance is precipitated. It may, however, be evaporated to dryness and re-dissolved in water without destruction of its activity, provided the temperature has not been allowed to rise too high.

We cannot doubt that substances of the nature of enzymes are generated abundantly in the tissues of both plants and animals, and that the secretions which are so intimately associated with the operations of digestion and other functions of the body, owe their special characters to the presence of peculiar substances of this order. There is also very little doubt that they are very similar in composition, in constitution, and in chemical properties, and probably they have a similar, or nearly similar, origin; but of their differences we know practically nothing, except by observation of their different

[1] *Berichte*, 1897, xxx. 117.

effects; and as to their origin and modes of action, there can be in the present state of knowledge nothing beyond conjecture. That they are also connected with the manifestation of disease there is great probability, and Jenner's great discovery and Pasteur's extension of the same principle, involving the use of attenuated or modified virus to neutralise the effects of the morbid secretions in the body, are doubtless dependent upon the special chemical effects of complex substances having the character of enzymes.

But here we reach the borderland where chemistry and physiology meet. Each has something to learn from the other. The chemist finds in the enzymes, which for the present are procurable only from the living organism which probably no laboratory synthesis will ever replace, agents which are often indispensable in his study of the more complex carbon compounds. The physiologist, on the other hand, must acknowledge that structural chemistry has given him the clue to many otherwise inexplicable transformations taking place in the body; while the pharmacologist and the physician, who are familiar with the history of the scientific labours of Pasteur from beginning to end, will admit that the discipline of the chemical laboratory is no bad preparation for the business of the scientific pathologist.

CHAPTER VII

THE ORIGIN OF STEREO-CHEMISTRY—CONSTITUTIONAL FORMULÆ IN SPACE

WHEN a ray of light passes through a crystal of Iceland spar it exhibits the familiar phenomenon of double refraction; that is to say, the ray in entering the crystal divides into two rays, which emerging separately, give rise to two distinct images. These two rays are *polarised* at right angles to each other. Light may also be polarised by reflection; in that case, one half the light is reflected, the other half passes into the reflecting surface, and is either stopped and ceases to produce the effect of light, or it is transmitted.

The discovery, however, which in connection with the subject about to be discussed possesses the greatest interest, was made early in the present century by the French physicist Biot. He found that a ray of light polarised in one plane has that plane twisted to the right or to the left in passing through certain substances of organic origin, such as sugar, camphor, and oil of turpentine when in the liquid state. He also observed that the angle of rotation of the plane of polarisation differs in different substances, and is directly proportional to the thickness of the layer of transparent substance through which the ray passes.

Now there are two classes of materials which have the power of rotating the polarised ray. One class, represented by quartz or sodium chlorate, are crystalline solids, and the optical power which they possess in the solid state is lost when they are liquefied by fusion or solution in a solvent. In such cases it would appear that the optical activity of the crystals is attributable to a peculiarity in the arrangement of their molecules one upon another, and not to any want of symmetry in the internal constitution of the molecules themselves. The other class includes those substances already mentioned, which exhibit their characteristic properties in the liquid state. In such cases it is fair to infer that the arrangement of the molecules has nothing to do with the phenomenon, which must be due to a peculiarity inherent in each molecule.

Common tartaric acid, obtained from the "tartar" deposited in the fermentation of wine, when dissolved in water rotates the polarised ray very strongly to the right. Its salts have the same property in different degrees. But the tartar got from grapes grown in certain districts (it was originally observed in tartar from the Vosges) yields an acid called racemic acid, which, while agreeing with tartaric acid in composition and in chemical properties, differs from it in being optically *inactive*, for a ray of polarised light passes through a solution of the acid, or of one of its salts, unaltered. Racemic acid, however, has been shown to consist of a mixture of two kinds of tartaric acid in equal quantities, and having equal but opposite effects on the polarised ray. Further, the property of rotating a polarised ray to the right or to the left is associated in crystallisable substances with a peculiarity of crystalline habit, in consequence of which they produce crystals, the fundamental form of which is modified by the development of small faces on one side or other of the crystals. When the sodium ammonium racemate is dissolved in water, and the solution is concentrated so as to deposit crystals, these crystals are found to be of two kinds, distinguished from each other by the position of the hemihedral faces referred to; some having these faces disposed on one side of the prism, and some—an equal number—on the opposite side, so that the two forms differ from each other only as an object differs from its image in a mirror, or as the right hand from the left. Consequently, such forms are not in any position superposable on one another. On separating these crystals, some will be found to agree with the crystals formed under similar circumstances from common tartaric acid, and like these, to turn the plane of polarisation to the right. The others having similar faces, but on the other side of the crystal, turn the plane of polarisation to the left, and the acid recovered from these crystals presents a corresponding property. Common tartaric acid, being called *dextro*-tartaric acid, the complementary compound is called *lævo*-tartaric acid; mixed together in equal quantities they reproduced racemic acid. Many similar cases are now known.

The discovery of all these important facts is due to Pasteur. Having been attracted at a very early age to the study of crystallography, he was led to repeat an examination of tartaric acid and the tartrates, published by De la Provostaye many years previously. In the first of a series of memoirs, in which he describes his observations and experiments on the relations subsisting between crystalline form, chemical composition, and direction of rotatory polarisation, he found that while common tartaric acid and all the common tartrates exhibit hemihedral forms in their crystals, and that the hemihedrism is always of the same kind, in paratartaric (racemic) acid and its salts hemihedral forms could not be detected. In the examination of these compounds he made the capital discovery already referred to. It will be worth while to quote his own words, written in 1848 : " Lorsque j'eus découvert l'hémiédrie de tous les tartrates je me hâtai d'étudier avec soin le paratartrate double de soude et d'ammoniaque ; mais je vis que les facettes tétraédriques correspondant à celles des tartrates isomorphes, étaient placées relativement aux faces principales du cristal, tantôt à droite, tantôt à gauche, sur les différents cristaux que j'avais obtenus. Prolongées respectivement ces facettes donnaient les deux tétraèdres symétriques dont nous parlions précédemment. Je séparai avec soin les cristaux hémièdres à droite, les cristaux hémièdres à gauche ; j'observai séparément leurs dissolutions dans l'appareil de polarisation de M. Biot, et je vis, avec surprise et bonheur que les cristaux hémièdres à gauche déviaient à gauche le plan de polarisation. . . . Les deux espèces de cristaux sont isomorphes et isomorphes avec le tartrate correspondant ; mais l'isomorphisme se présente là avec une particularité jusqu'ici sans exemple ; c'est l'isomorphism de deux cristaux dissymétriques qui se regardent dans un miroir." [1]

Pasteur was, of course, not content to let his investigations stop here. He proceeded to investigate the questions whether the connection between rotatory polarisation and hemihedral crystallisation are in all cases connected together ; in fact, whether from observation of the one property the other may always be predicted. These inquiries led him to the experimental study of a number of substances other than the tartaric acids, among the rest the important vegetable principle asparagine, which is obtainable from the juice of a number of plants, such as asparagus, marshmallow, and various species of leguminosæ, especially, as shown by Pasteur, the juice of vetches blanched by exclusion of daylight. Having assured himself of the hemihedrism of the crystals of asparagine, Pasteur proceeded to examine

[1] *Ann. Chim.*, 3rd series, xxiv. 456 (1848).

the action of a solution of this substance on the polarised ray, and found that when dissolved in water or alkalis it deviates the plane of polarisation to the left. At this time only one kind of asparagine was known, but so confident was Pasteur in his belief in the correctness of the principles deduced from his observations on tartaric acid, that he did not hesitate to predict the discovery of a complementary dextro-rotatory form, such that between these two kinds of asparagine the same relation would be found to exist as between right- and left-handed tartaric acid.[1] Dextro-rotatory and inactive asparagine have, in fact, been since discovered. In the examination of one of the formates, the strontium salt, he encountered a different phenomenon. In this case, while the crystals exhibit hemihedrism, the two opposite forms are always simultaneously produced; and when the crystals are separated, neither the right-hand nor the left-hand form dissolved in water exhibits any rotatory power. Moreover, while the dextro-tartrate or lævo-tartrate, when recrystallised, never yield crystals of the opposite form, the formate, whether dextro or lævo, always gives a mixture of both kinds of crystal.[2] The explanation of the difference between these two cases was supplied by Pasteur himself. He says,[3] "Les faits précédents conduisent à supposer que l'hémiédrie du

---

[1] *Ann. Chim.*, 3rd series, xxxi. 72 (1851).
[2] *Ann. Chim.*, 3rd series, xxxi. 100 (1851).
[3] *Loc. cit.*, p. 101.

formiate de strontiane ne tient pas à l'arrangement des atomes dans la molécule chimique, mais à l'arrangement des molécules physiques dans le cristal total, de telle manière que la structure cristalline une fois disparue dans l'acte de la dissolution il n'y a plus de dissymétrie; à peu près comme si l'on construisait un édifice ayant la forme extérieure d'un polyèdre qui offrirait *l'hémiédrie non superposable* et que l'on détruirait ensuite."

It appears, then, that if a substance in the liquid form possesses the power of rotating the polarised ray, it will produce in crystallising hemihedral forms[1] which are not superposable, and which have the mutual relation of an object and its image as seen in a mirror. On the other hand, optical activity cannot be inferred for the liquid state from the existence of hemihedral crystalline forms.

The first to perceive the connection between all these phenomena and the question as to the internal structure of molecules possessing such peculiarities was Pasteur himself; and so far back as 1853 he was able to anticipate to some extent the views accepted later by all chemists. If in two substances composed of the same elements, united in the same

---

[1] In some of these cases the hemihedral form only makes its appearance when a particular condition is established in the solution. Thus Pasteur himself showed that calcium bimalate crystallises in hemihedral forms from nitric acid but not from water.— *Ann. Chim.*, 3rd series, xxxviii. 437 (1853).

proportions, and having the same chemical properties, we can perceive only the two differences already described (*i.e.* direction of rotation and hemihedral crystallisation), and in many cases only one of them, namely, the optical activity, we are driven to the conclusion that their peculiarities must be connected with some peculiarity of construction in the molecule. The atoms composing the molecule in one of these compounds must be arranged in some way which is repeated in the other, but *in inverse order*, so that the two would be related in the same way as an object and its image in a mirror. "Are the atoms of the dextro-acid grouped on the spirals of a right-handed helix, or placed at the solid angles of an irregular tetrahedron, or disposed according to some particular asymmetric arrangement?" If dextro- or lævo-tartaric acid is combined with some substance, such as potash, ammonia, aniline, which is inactive, and hence devoid of asymmetry, the inactive substance affects to the same extent the activity of both varieties of the acid; but if the two acids are combined with an active substance, such as the alkaloid cinchonine, Pasteur found that a pair of compounds results which differ in form, in solubility, and in other properties. While in the one case the rotatory power is the sum of the rotatory powers of the acid and the base, in the other case the rotatory power of the compound is the difference between the two. On these facts Pasteur based a method which has been since freely employed for the separation of the constituents of racemoid compounds. If racemic acid, for example, be saturated with the active base cinchonicine, the first crystals obtained from the solution consist of pure cinchonicine lævo-tartrate, while the whole of the dextro-tartrate remains in the mother liquor, and can afterwards be obtained in forms distinct from those of the lævo-tartrate.

The ideas put forth quite clearly, but in general terms, by Pasteur were long afterwards developed into a definite theory of structure, which forms the foundation of that large department or aspect of our science which is called *Stereo-chemistry*, or chemistry in space of three dimensions.

But while the merit of creating the basis of this system of ideas, by providing the facts and showing clearly the direction in which further investigation should travel, belongs to Pasteur, it is only just to recall the fact that the necessity for a theory of the kind was perceived long before Pasteur's researches gave the clue which led ultimately to the conception of the doctrine of symmetry and asymmetry in carbon compounds.

The fundamental idea of stereo-chemistry arises immediately out of the doctrine of atoms. Dalton himself and others of his time, promoters of the atomic system, were led to consider, though without giving the subject much attention, the question of the arrangement which united atoms must occupy in space. Dalton's diagrams ("Chemical Philosophy," Part I.) represent all the atoms lying in one plane, but the question was raised very definitely by Wollaston, so early as 1808, at the conclusion of a paper in which he brought forward experiments in support of the atomic doctrine.[1] He says, "I am further inclined to think that when our views are sufficiently extended to enable us to reason with precision concerning the proportions of elementary atoms, we shall find the arithmetical relation alone will not be sufficient to explain their mutual action, and that we shall be obliged to acquire a geometrical conception of their relative arrangement in all the three dimensions of solid extension." But after giving some examples of possible arrangements, he goes on to say that as this geometrical arrangement of the primary elements of matter is altogether conjectural, it must rely for its confirmation or rejection upon future inquiry, and he adds, "It is perhaps too much to hope that the geometrical arrangement of primary particles will ever be perfectly known."

Leopold Gmelin seems to have been more inclined to be hopeful, for in 1848 we find in his great "Handbook of Organic Chemistry" (vol. i., *Cavendish Society Publications*): "Suggestions respecting the Relative Position of the Elementary Atoms in a Compound Organic Atom, assuming the

---

[1] "On Superacid and Subacid Salts," by William Hyde Wollaston (*Phil. Trans.*, xcviii. (1808), pp. 96–102). Reprinted by Alembic Club, No. 2.

truth of the Nucleus Theory." "Nearly all chemists," he says, "adopt the Atomic Theory. They determine the relative weights of the atoms, and their relative distances one from the other, or the relative space occupied by each atom of the combined substances, including the surrounding calorific envelope; hypotheses are also made respecting the form of the atoms, &c. Why, then, should we not likewise throw out suggestions with regard to their relative positions?" This he proceeds to do, and with the aid of certain *à priori* principles, he arrives at the conclusion that potassium sulphate, for example, must have the form of a double four-sided pyramid, that ethylene has probably the form of a cube, alcohol and acetic acid other forms. All these forms, however, require the assumption of a certain number of atoms in each molecule which would be dependent upon the atomic weights assigned to each. As these have in many cases been changed since Gmelin's time, his assumptions necessarily fall to the ground; but the arguments employed are interesting, as affording an example of an early and serious attempt to attack problems of this kind. At the conclusion of the discussion he continues as follows: "Even if the data of this investigation are defective or erroneous, I am yet convinced that all theories on the constitution of organic compounds, and all controversies as to this or that mode of writing rational formulæ, if not supported by a plausible arrangement of the compound atom, will aid us but little in the acquisition of correct ideas. Look, for instance, at the controversy respecting the constitution of ether and alcohol between Dumas and Boullay on the one side, and Berzelius and Liebig on the other. According to the former, ether is a compound of etherine with water $= C_4H_4 Aq$, and alcohol $= C_4H_4 2Aq$; according to the latter, the hypothetical radical ethyl $= C_4H_5$ forms with O the oxide of ethyl = ether; and this with the addition of 1At. water forms the hydrated oxide of ethyl $=$ alcohol $= C_4H_5O + Aq$. Now, on comparing these views with the explanation given, it appears probable that neither of them is right. At all events, neither ether nor alcohol can be supposed to contain water ready formed. They are not hydrates; if so, they would surely give up this water to burnt lime or baryta, which, however, is not the case. Neither is ether converted into alcohol by solution in water. On the other hand, ethyl is a fictitious compound, supposed to combine like a metal with oxygen and with chlorine, forming compounds analogous to the metallic oxides and chlorides. Thus hydrochloric ether $= C_4H_5Cl$ ($= C_4H_3Cl, H_2.Gm$) is regarded as chloride of ethyl; but it does not precipitate silver solutions, &c."

Long afterwards, in 1872, the study of the lactic acids led Wislicenus again to perceive that the then existing conceptions of atoms and their union together were insufficient to explain the facts, and to suggest that they might be accounted for "durch verschiedene Lagerung ihrer Atome im Raume."[1] But there the matter rested till the theory of Van't Hoff and Le Bel was enunciated two years later.[2] What Van't Hoff and Le Bel discovered was the remarkable fact that, in carbon compounds which exhibit the property of rotating the polarised ray in either direction, the molecule in every case contains at least one atom of carbon combined in four different ways; that is, having its four units of valency occupied with radicles of different composition, and therefore usually of different combining weights. Thus in succinic acid, an example of an optically inactive compound, there are four atoms of carbon, the affinities of which are disposed of according to the order displayed in the following diagram :—

SUCCINIC ACID.

$$\begin{array}{c} \text{O H H O} \\ \| | | \| \\ \text{H—O—C—C—C—C—O—H} \\ | | \\ \text{H H} \end{array}$$

In chloro-succinic acid, we have a compound in which the carbon atoms are linked together in the

[1] Ann. Chim., clxvi. 3, clxvii. 302, 346.
[2] Voorstel tot uitbreiding der structuurformules in de ruimte, pamphlet published by J. H. Van't Hoff, Sept. 1874 : republished under the title Sur les formules de structure dans l'espace. Archives Neerland, ix., 1874, pp. 445–454 ; Bulletin Soc. Chim., Paris, xxiii., 1875, pp. 295–301.
Sur les relations qui existent entre les formules atomiques des corps organiques, et le pouvoir rotatoire de leurs dissolutions. By J. A. Le Bel, Bulletin Soc. Chim., Paris, xxii., 1874, pp. 337–347.

same order, but one of them has exchanged an atom of hydrogen for an atom of chlorine—

CHLORO-SUCCINIC ACID.

$$\begin{array}{ccccccc} & O & H & Cl & O & \\ & \| & | & | & \| & \\ H-O-C-&C-&C-&C-&O-H \\ & | & | & & & \\ & H & H & & & \end{array}$$

In this molecule, then, one atom of carbon is attached to four different atoms or groups, for it is united to (1) H, (2) (Cl), (3) CH_2, and (4) CO.O. This compound is known in two optically active forms, which show the same kind of relation to each other which has already been observed in the case of tartaric acid.

Tartaric acid itself contains two atoms of carbon in the same kind of condition, each united with (1) H, (2) OH, (3) CH_2, and (4) CO.O. To explain the effect of this upon the optical properties of the compound, a further hypothesis is required. In all the early speculations regarding the nature of atoms, it seems to have been assumed, as it was by Dalton and Wollaston, that the "virtual extent" of each atom is spherical. Since that day several other hypotheses have been suggested concerning the nature of the atom, of which one of the most important is Lord Kelvin's notion of *vortices;* and it will be obvious to every one who considers the subject, that our views of the process of chemical combination must be seriously affected by the idea in the mind of the form and nature of the atoms supposed to be in the act of union.

The idea which has proved most fertile is one which appeared for the first time in a paper by Kekulé in 1867.[1] At that time he was still engaged in the elaboration of the great doctrine of the linking of atoms, of which, as already shown (Chap. V.), we owe the chief development to his insight. And the use of models, as well as of "graphic" formulæ, was beginning to be freely practised by the more advanced chemists. At the end of a paper on the constitution of mesitylene, in a kind of supplementary note, Kekulé pointed out that the models then most in favour, consisting of spherical balls joined together by rods, were no better than diagrams, since it was impossible to display combination between two atoms by more than one unit of valency; and, moreover, everything was represented as lying in the same plane. But by using a sphere to represent the atom of carbon, and four rods to represent its four affinities, *placed in the directions of four hexhedral axes ending in the faces of a tetrahedron,* these difficulties could be got over, and two such models placed together could be used to represent union by one, two, or three units. Van't Hoff adopted and has pursued with most brilliant success the consequences of this remarkable idea.[2]

[1] *Zeitschrift f. Chem.* (1867), N.F. iii. 217.
[2] For details concerning the verification of the theory, and the removal of difficulties in its way, arising chiefly out of erroneous observations, see Van't Hoff's *Dix Anneés dans l'histoire d'une Théorie*, of which an English edition has been prepared by Mr. J. E. Marsh. Clarendon Press.

An atom of carbon, then, is generally believed to be capable of combining with *four* other atoms and no more, and is therefore said to be tetrad or quadrivalent. The carbon atom is supposed by this hypothesis to be accessible only in four different directions, which are representable by the four straight lines which may be drawn from the centre of a regular tetrahedron to its solid angles. The centre of mass of the carbon atom is supposed to be situated at the intersection of these lines, or at the centre of the figure. A model to represent such an arrangement could be easily made by means of a ball of wood and four wires of equal length. If two such models be constructed, and the wires marked by tipping them with beads of different colours, or in some other way, it can easily be shown that two distinct arrangements become possible. In the following figures the letters *a, b, c, d* represent the atoms, all different, which we may imagine to be united, as in chloro-succinic acid, to the same atom of carbon:—

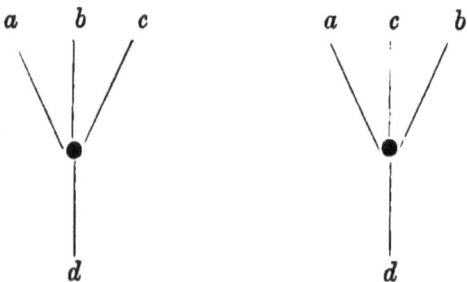

A consideration of these figures will show that the one is not superposable upon the other so that the same letters come together. Any change in the plane of polarisation produced by one of these structures would be also produced, but in the inverse sense, by the other structure. The exact mechanism of this process cannot at present be described, because we have no more positive knowledge as to the construction of a molecule than we have of the atoms composing it. Pasteur, as already stated, frequently used the analogy of a spiral with a twist to the right or to the left, according as the molecule possessed dextro- or lævo-rotatory powers.

The use of models assists materially in the consideration of the problems arising out of this hypothesis. One of the first questions which arise relates to the direction in which the several valencies of an atom of carbon may be supposed to be exerted. If the direction of these be supposed to be absolutely fixed, then it can be shown that (1) two carbon atoms cannot unite by two bonds, nor by three, because that would involve the distortion of the atom; and (2) three or more carbon atoms cannot unite to form a ring, for the same reason.

Hence it seems that if the direction of the attractions of carbon for other atoms can be determined at all, the line of attraction must be rather easily displaceable from the normal, or it operates somewhat like the pole of a magnet, that is, there is a certain *field*. The analogy between the attractions of two atoms for each other, and the attraction exercised between the opposite poles of two magnets, or between a magnet and a piece of iron, may in fact be considered as extending even further. For just as the presence of a mass of iron in the neighbourhood of a magnetic pole seems to absorb the lines of magnetic induction and so reduce the action of the magnet upon other bodies placed near, so the addition of one element to another in chemical union diminishes the tendency of either to combine with a third element, but does not, in the majority of cases, absolutely extinguish this tendency. Hence we have what has been called "residual valency," which, whatever may be the fate of the various hypotheses concerning it, gives rise to very well marked phenomena of combination. It is, however, usually believed that two carbon atoms may actually be united by two or more units of valency, but that in all such cases the combination is not only not more secure, but is decidedly more easily broken up than where one bond only of each is employed. To account for this difference, so contrary to what might be at first sight expected, two chief hypotheses have been proposed. The first, which originated with Von Baeyer,[1] is based upon the same hypothesis with regard to the carbon atom as that of Le Bel and Van't Hoff. If the valencies of the carbon atom act along the lines drawn from the centre to the solid angles of the regular tetrahedron, these lines form with each other angles of 109° 28'. If two carbon atoms are so situated towards each

[1] *Ber.*, xviii. 2277.

other that two valencies of each are united together so that the directions of the two are parallel to each other, each is turned out of its normal position by an angle of 54° 44'; and if two carbon atoms are similarly joined by three units of valency, each of these must deviate 70° 32' from its normal position. It is known that combination by double or triple bonds is easily converted into union by single bonds in all cases of this kind. Such substances as acetylene and ethylene are saturated with great readiness, not only by bromine, but by hydracids, and even by iodine, and the tension is thus relieved.

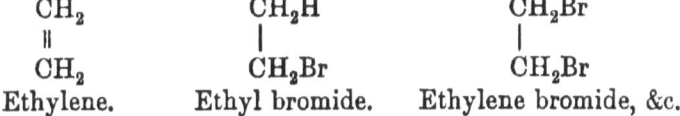

$$\begin{array}{ccc} \text{CH}_2 & \text{CH}_2\text{H} & \text{CH}_2\text{Br} \\ \| & | & | \\ \text{CH}_2 & \text{CH}_2\text{Br} & \text{CH}_2\text{Br} \\ \text{Ethylene.} & \text{Ethyl bromide.} & \text{Ethylene bromide, \&c.} \end{array}$$

V. Baeyer has also pointed out that in the formation of rings of carbon atoms the distortion of the atoms diminishes as the number of carbon atoms increases up to five. In a ring of six carbon atoms united by single bonds the distortion is a little greater. The following angles represent the extent to which the direction of each valency is disturbed:—

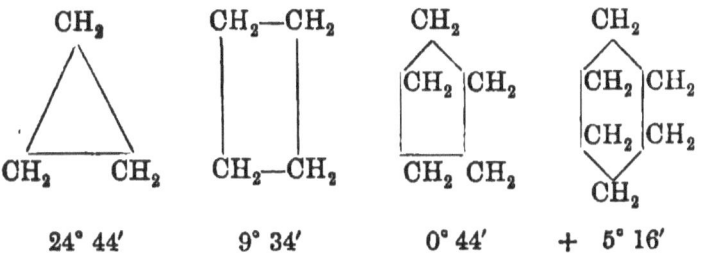

24° 44'   9° 34'   0° 44'   + 5° 16'

The other hypothesis, proposed by Wunderlich,[1] is based upon the idea that the relative force of attraction between two units of valency depends upon the relative distances through which they have to act. Briefly, the hypothesis is somewhat as follows. The carbon atom is a sphere from which four equal symmetrically placed segments have been removed, and the circular faces thus formed are situated in the planes of the four faces of a regular tetrahedron. When combination takes place between two carbon atoms the most intimate union is that in which two of these faces are placed parallel to, and probably very near, each other. A less intimate union occurs when the centres of gravity of two faces of one atom attracts two faces of another. The two tetrahedra have then a common edge, the two pairs of faces forming equal angles with each other. And, lastly, three faces of one may attract equally three faces of the other, and so cause the two tetrahedra to be applied to each other by one of their solid angles. These three positions correspond to combination by single, double, and triple bonds.

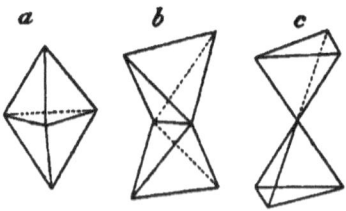

[1] *Configuration Organischer Moleküle*, Würtzburg, 1886. Abstract in *Ber.*, xix. 592c.

According to this assumption it is only possible for the atoms to touch each other when united by the single bond, as shown at a.

When two asymmetric carbon atoms are united together the number of possible isomeric forms is greater. Tartaric acid is a case of this kind. Four isomeric acids of the same composition are known, namely: dextro-tartaric acid, lævo-tartaric, meso-tartaric, and racemic acids. Racemic acid is known by the researches of Pasteur, made forty years ago, to consist of a mixture or molecular compound of dextro- and lævo-tartaric acids. These two latter are supposed to be related to each other in the manner indicated in the following formulæ:—

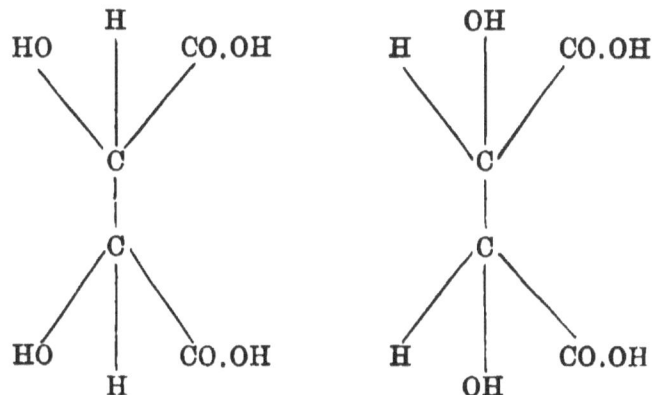

which may be more briefly written:

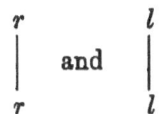

where the letters r and l represent an arrangement which results in right- or left-handed rotation of the polarised ray. Meso-tartaric acid, which, as already explained, is optically inactive, though containing two asymmetric carbons, is by an extension of the same hypothesis represented as

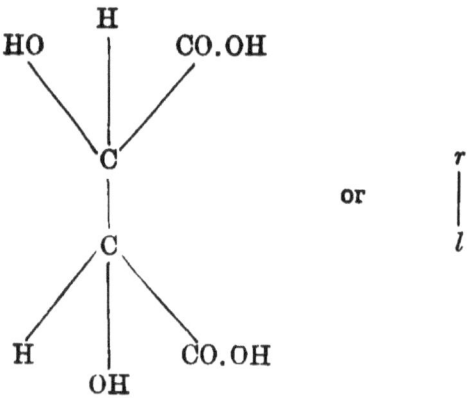

Van't Hoff long ago indicated that when two carbon atoms are united together by a single bond they may be supposed to be free to rotate about an axis which is in the line representing the direction of the uniting valencies, and that if two carbons are joined by two or more bonds rotation becomes impossible. This hypothesis was first made use of by Wislicenus in 1886, and has been the subject of a good deal of discussion since.

It may be assumed that the radicles united to two adjacent atoms of carbon will be likely to influence each other,[1] and, according as they attract or repel each other, rotation may or may not occur. Thus it may be supposed that in Dutch liquid the

[1] The relative masses (atomic weights) of the atoms or atomic groups may have something to do with this.

chlorine and hydrogen atoms probably attract each other. Hence there can be only one stable form of this compound, viz. :—

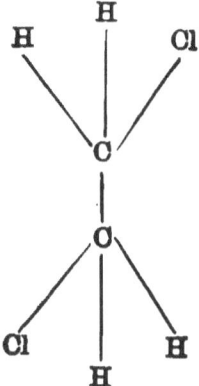

other arrangements passing spontaneously by rotation into this.[1] Succinic acid also is known in only one form, which probably has the following structure :—

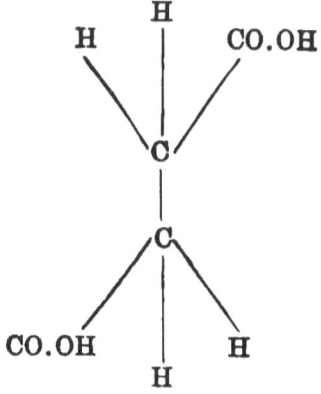

---

[1] That atoms which are not directly united do influence each other is certain from such cases as the O of the carboxyl group – CO.OH, the characters of bromnitroethane, the chloranilines, &c.

If this be so, it seems to follow that rotation must occur when water is lost and the anhydride is formed under the influence of heat :—

$$\begin{array}{c} \overset{H}{\underset{}{|}} \\ \overset{H}{}\underset{|}{\overset{}{C}}-C=O \\ |\!\!\diagdown\!O \\ \underset{|}{C}-C=O \\ \overset{H}{}\underset{H}{} \end{array}$$

From other similar cases it appears probable that the formation of rings, in which four carbon atoms, or four carbon atoms and one oxygen atom are concerned, probably occurs in one plane. And Von Baeyer has pointed out that the interior angles of a regular pentagon are very nearly equal to the angle which the valencies of carbon in their normal position form with one another (see diagram, p. 199). This appears to explain such facts as the ready production of anhydrides from dibasic acids, such as succinic acid, already referred to, and phthalic acid, &c.; also the formation of lactones by loss of the elements of water by the γ hydroxy-acids of the fatty series, such as oxybutyric acid. It is certainly interesting to compare the action of heat upon a β acid with that of a γ acid of the same series; for example :—

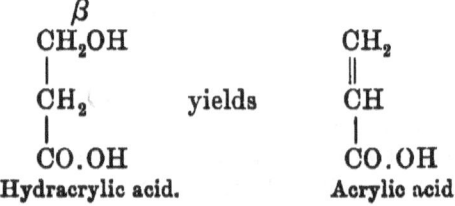

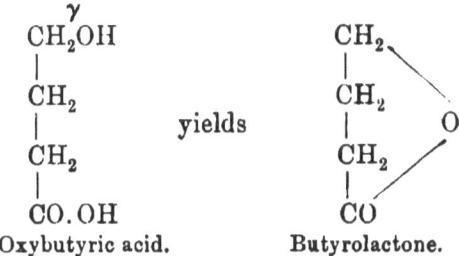

Oxybutyric acid.   Butyrolactone.

One or two other questions relating to the origin or constitution of optically active bodies have been the subject of discussion and much experiment. As they are still unsettled, they may be dismissed briefly. Attempts have been made to trace a relation between the degree or *amount* of rotation produced by a compound and the *masses* of the radicles which enter into its composition in union with the asymmetric carbon atom it contains. It has been found in some cases which have been examined that two of the four groups may have the same weight, and yet the compound is still active. Guye therefore supposes[1] that not merely the masses of the atomic groups but their relative distances from the carbon to which they are attached may influence the rotatory power. Some regularities which seem to support these views have actually been observed by Guye; but on the other hand there are many cases which are incompatible with them.

There appears to be some reason for thinking that it may be possible to trace the effect of each

[1] *Compt. Rend.* (1893), cxvi. 1451.

constituent of an optically active body upon its rotatory power, but at present no determinations have been placed on record which are sufficient to set the question at rest.[1] It would appear probable that this problem will assume and retain for a long time the position and aspect presented by the somewhat similar questions which arise in connection with many of the physical characters of chemical compounds. The specific or molecular volumes of liquids and solids, their magnetic rotation, their refractive power, and even their boiling points, may each be represented by numerical values which are respectively the sum of terms which are nearly but not absolutely constant, and which may be attributed to the several constituents of the compound. But just as it is impossible even now to assign an invariable value to the specific volume, for example, of an elementary atom, so it is not very likely that the specific rotation produced by a particular asymmetric group of atoms will be found constant; and in both cases for the same reason, namely, that notwithstanding the accepted doctrine of atom-linking, based on the idea of valency, there can be no doubt that in a molecule every atom exerts an influence, greater or less, on every other atom.

Closely connected with the inquiry as to the effect upon the plane of polarisation of the constituent radicles in a compound is another which has arisen

[1] See J. W. Walker, *Jour. Chem. Soc.* (1895), lxvii. 914.

out of the researches of Walden. Compounds which contain asymmetric carbon, and hence are capable of existing in two stereo-isomeric forms, when produced from inactive materials by ordinary laboratory processes, invariably appear in the racemic condition; that is, an equal quantity of each oppositely active variety is produced. It now appears, however, that starting from one and the same active compound, a given derivative formed from it may exhibit a rotatory power the same or the reverse of that of the parent substance. From *lævo*-malic acid, according to Walden,[1] is produced by the action of pentachloride of phosphorus, a chloro-succinic acid which is *dextro*-rotatory. Replacing the chlorine in this compound by hydroxyl, a malic acid is reproduced, which is also *dextro*-rotatory. This malic acid, treated with phosphorus pentachloride, gives *lævo*-chloro-succinic acid, from which *lævo*-malic acid identical with the original substance may be regenerated. Phosphoric chloride appears therefore to have a peculiar power in such cases of causing optical inversion, by which it is distinguished from all other reagents. Natural *lævo*-asparagine and the aspartic acid formed from it yield, by the action of nitrosyl chloride, *lævo*-chloro-succinic acid;[2] while, as stated above, the malic acid derived from the same substances yields, by the action of phosphoric chloride, a chloro-succinic acid

[1] *Ber.*, xxix. 133 (1896).
[2] Tilden and Marshall, *Jour. Chem. Soc.*, lxvii. 494 (1895).

of opposite sign. Walden's production of optical antipodes may be represented by the following diagram :—

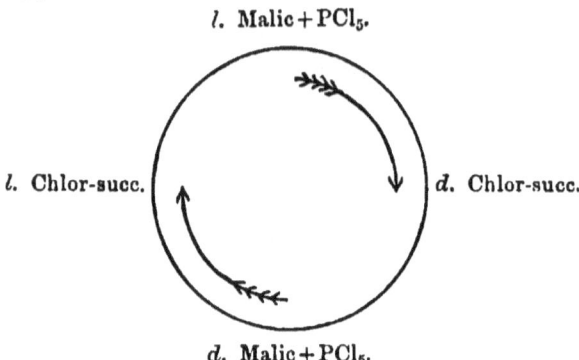

The hypotheses of which an outline has been given relate to the atom of the element carbon; but considerations of this kind, if valid in the case of one element, must be applicable to others. Hitherto, however, but little progress has been made in this direction, for no other element is yet known which possesses equally with carbon the power of uniting with other atoms of the same kind (*i.e.* carbon to carbon, &c.), and at the same time of combining with several different atoms forming compounds which exhibit optical activity or some other manifestation of asymmetry.

CHAPTER VIII

ELECTRICITY AND CHEMICAL AFFINITY

IN the *Philosophical Transactions* for 1784 will be found a paper by the Hon. Henry Cavendish, which embodies those results of his " Experiments on Air " which led to the famous discovery of the composition of water. The proposition that water consists or is composed of two elementary gases is, however, all the more firmly established when, to the statement of Cavendish that from two measures of " inflammable air " (hydrogen) exploded with one measure of " dephlogisticated air " (oxygen) water is produced, we are in a position to add that from the decomposition of water these two gases, and nothing else, can be reproduced. This latter result was observed for the first time by Nicholson and Carlisle in 1800, only sixteen years later than the announcement of Cavendish's discovery.

In the meantime a new philosophical instrument and a new field of research had been brought within the reach of chemists and physicists by the discoveries of Galvani and Volta, which culminated in the invention of the Voltaic Pile and the Voltaic Battery shortly before this time. Electric currents could thus be procured at will, and the voltaic decomposition of acidified water was followed by a host of observations of a similar kind. Solutions of various salts submitted to the action of the current yielded in some cases acids and alkalis, in others acid and oxygen at one pole, while metal and hydrogen appeared at the opposite pole. By this same agency Davy, in 1807, succeeded in proving that potash and soda are oxides containing a pair of very remarkable metals.

The attention of chemists in this way became attracted to the fascinating phenomena of electrolytic or electro-chemical decomposition, and not only were many facts discovered of greater or less practical utility, but hypotheses were necessarily framed to account for the facts. Davy himself, after some years occupied more or less with the study of the galvanic phenomena, seems to have arrived at the conclusion that chemical combination is produced by the union of atoms charged with opposite kinds of electricity; and, in fact, to have identified chemical "affinity" with electrical attraction between particles, or, at any rate, to have regarded chemical affinity and electrical attraction as dependent upon the same cause. A similar theory was formulated by Berzelius about 1818, but the Swedish chemist considered it probable that "simple and compound atoms are electro-polar; in the majority of them one of the poles is endowed with a preponderant force, the intensity of which varies according to the nature of the body. Those in which the + pole is preponderant are called electro-positive, those in which the − pole predominates are electro-negative."[1] Hence, according to Berzelius, each atom contains both positive and negative electricity; but the atom of oxygen, for example, has a large amount of negative electricity accumulated upon one pole, with a relatively small amount of positive electricity at the other, while the atom of such an element as potassium possesses a strong charge of positive with a small charge of negative electricity. During the act of combination the positive pole of one atom is turned toward the negative pole of the atom with which it is about to unite, and the opposite electricities neutralise each other with production of the phenomena of heat and light, as in the production of sparks between oppositely charged masses.

From this time forward little further progress was made, so far as electro-chemical phenomena were concerned, till the subject was taken up by Faraday about 1832; and as the result of his researches the two important quantitative statements which are usually known as Faraday's Laws of Electrolysis, together with a vast body of other important observations, were established. The statements referred to may, for the sake of completeness, be recalled to the recollection of the reader. The first of these may be given in the original words of

[1] Berzelius, *Traité de Chimie*, vol. i. (1842).

the discoverer: "The chemical power of a current of electricity is in direct proportion to the absolute quantity of electricity which passes."[1] Faraday's own language may also be used to lead up to and express the second law. "Compound bodies," he says,[2] "may be separated into two great classes, namely, those which are decomposible by the electric current and those which are not. Of the latter some are conductors, others non-conductors, of voltaic electricity. . . . I propose to call bodies of the decomposible class *electrolytes*. Then, again, the substances into which these divide, under the influence of the electric current, form an exceedingly important general class. They are combining bodies, are directly associated with the fundamental parts of the doctrine of chemical affinity, and have each a definite proportion in which they are always evolved during electrolytic action. I have proposed to call these bodies generally *ions*, or particularly *anions* and *cations*, according as they appear at the *anode* or *cathode*, and the numbers representing the proportions in which they are evolved *electro-chemical equivalents*. Thus oxygen, chlorine, iodine, hydrogen, lead, tin, are *ions*; the three former are *anions*, hydrogen and the two metals are *cations*, and 8, 36, 125, 1, 104, 58, are their electro-chemical equivalents nearly."[3] We learn from this, and from other

[1] "Experimental Researches in Electricity," vol. i. p. 241.
[2] *Loc. cit.*, pp. 242, 243.
[3] In this passage there is in the original a slight verbal slip, which is corrected above.

experiments described in the course of these researches, that the electro-chemical equivalents of ions are the same as their ordinary chemical equivalents or combining proportions.

Faraday's view as to the cause of electrolytic phenomena led him to reject the notion entertained by some of his predecessors that electro-chemical decomposition was the result of the electrical attraction or repulsion of the poles acting upon the constituents of the electrolyte. He states expressly that he believed that the effect is due to a force acting internally upon the ions, and "either superadded to or giving direction to the ordinary chemical affinity of the bodies present."

Nevertheless, while correcting some of the experimental errors in Davy's work, Faraday seems to have entertained nearly the same idea with regard to the nature of the phenomena of chemical combination and electro-chemical decomposition, for (*loc. cit.*, p. 248) he refers, with evident sympathy, to "the beautiful idea that ordinary chemical affinity is a mere consequence of the electrical attractions of the particles of different kinds of matter"; and a little further on he states his "conviction that the power which governs electro-chemical decomposition and ordinary chemical attractions is the same." This idea evidently became established in the mind of Faraday, for in a later paper[1] the following passage occurs: "All the

[1] "Experimental Researches in Electricity," vol. i. p. 272.

facts show us that that power commonly called chemical affinity can be communicated to a distance through the metals and certain forms of carbon; that the electric current is only another form of the forces of chemical affinity; that its power is in proportion to the chemical affinities producing it; that when it is deficient in force it may be helped by calling in chemical aid, the want in the former being made up by an equivalent of the latter; that in other words *the forces termed chemical affinity and electricity are one and the same.*" This view was adopted by other writers. Daniell, for example, the inventor of the constant cell, in his " Chemical Philosophy," heads the paragraphs relating to the battery by the title, " Circulating Affinity or Electricity."

The phenomena of electro-chemical decomposition present a great many questions of difficulty, the interpretation of which have led in the past and are likely still to lead to much difference of opinion and controversy. When, for example, an electric current is sent through a solution of copper sulphate, the ordinary visible products which accumulate at the poles are metallic copper at the cathode, and oxygen gas at the anode. If the current is strong, hydrogen is also given off with the copper. When sodium sulphate is used instead of copper sulphate, the products are gaseous hydrogen and oxygen; while the solution, originally neutral, becomes alkaline from the production of soda round the cathode, and acid from the accumulation of sulphuric acid round the anode. The difference between these two results has been explained in the terms of two distinct hypotheses, the earlier of which was based on the dualistic theory of salts. In the system inaugurated by Lavoisier, and approved by Berzelius, every salt was made up of two oxides— the one of a metal, the other of a non-metal; thus cupric sulphate was supposed to consist of copper oxide united to sulphur trioxide or sulphuric acid, while sodium sulphate was composed of soda or oxide of sodium united to the same sulphuric acid. Expressed in symbols, they stood thus :—

Cupric sulphate . . . . $CuO.SO_3$
Sodium sulphate . . . . $NaO.SO_3$

Berzelius and his school supposed that when these compounds are decomposed by the electric current the ions are CuO and SO_3 in one case, and NaO and SO_3 in the other; but that in the case of the copper salt the metal separates in consequence of the simultaneous decomposition of water, the hydrogen of which reduces the metallic oxide uniting with the oxygen and setting the metal free.

The other hypothesis was based on the unitary system, of which the germ perhaps may be found in the writings of Davy, but which was formally introduced by Daniell about 1842,[1] and afterwards adopted by Gerhardt upon evidence of a different

[1] Daniell's "Chemical Philosophy," 2nd edit. pp. 432-440.

kind. According to this view the two salts are resolved on electrolysis into the ions Cu and SO_4, Na and SO_4 respectively. The decomposition of the copper compound therefore gives metal as the primary cation, while at the anode the radicle SO_4 is resolved into O, which escapes, and SO_3, which forms sulphuric acid with the water. In the case of the sodium salt, the alkali and the acid observed are alike *secondary* products; the former resulting from the action of the liberated sodium upon the water with simultaneous escape of hydrogen gas.

Another question which required investigation relates to the course of the current through the solution. It is a remarkable fact that water alone appears to be almost destitute of conducting power, its resistance increasing in proportion as it is more free from dissolved salts or gases. But the addition of a very small quantity of sulphuric acid seems to make it not only conduct freely, but undergo electrochemical decomposition into its constituents oxygen and hydrogen. When the current passes, is it really conveyed by the water, by the acid, or by some compound of the two? That is a very important question; but in order to supply the answer to it, which is provided by commonly received theories of the present day, it is necessary to know something of the course of observation and experiment which has led within the last ten years to the adoption of rather remarkable views concerning the state of dissolved electrolytes, and the nature of solutions generally.

So long ago as 1788 Sir Charles Blagden published in the *Philosophical Transactions* a paper dealing with the familiar fact that salt water does not freeze so easily as fresh water. In that paper he showed that various salts added to water cause a depression of the freezing point, and that the depression is in each case practically proportional to the amount of the salt present. There the question remained for nearly a century. The next steps in advance could only be taken when Blagden's conclusions had been established upon a much firmer basis of exact experiment than he had been able to supply; and, as in so many other cases, it required the successive efforts of many experimenters to provide material upon which to build theory with any prospect of success. Among the workers who took up the question must be mentioned Rüdorff,[1] De Coppet,[2] and Guthrie.[3] De Coppet got so far as to show that the "co-efficient of depression" of the freezing point is constant for the same substance, and that it is equal for similar substances when added to the same quantity of water in amounts proportional to their molecular weights. It is, however, to the important researches of Professor F. M. Raoult[4] of Grenoble that the

[1] *Pogg.*, cxiv. 63 (1861), cxvi. 55 (1862), &c.
[2] *Ann. Chim.*, xxiii. 366 (1871), xxv. 502 (1872), xxvi. 98 (1872).
[3] *Phil. Mag.*, 1875, 1876, 1878.
[4] *Ann. Chim.*, xxviii. 133 (1883), &c.

establishment of this generalisation is due, and as a result a new method has been provided for the determination of the molecular weights of those substances to which the vapour-density method is not applicable. Raoult's law may be stated as follows: the depression of the freezing point of a liquid, caused by the solution in it of a liquid or solid, is proportional to the absolute amount of dissolved substance, and is inversely proportional to its molecular weight. Consequently, if a number of different substances be taken in the proportions of their molecular weights, and dissolved in a liquid which is capable of solidifying at a determinable temperature, the resulting reduction of the freezing point will be the same in each case. This molecular depression is then a constant for any given liquid, though of course it differs in different liquids. The solvents recommended by Raoult are water, acetic acid, and benzene. If we take A as the reduction of freezing point caused by the solution of 1 gram of substance in 100 grams of water, for example, M the molecular weight of the substance, and T the lowering of the freezing point caused by the solution of a molecular proportion of the substance in 100 parts of liquid, then, if the solution is dilute,

$$MA = T.$$

The value of T for water has been found to be 19 in reference to a great variety of neutral carbon compounds, but it rises to about 37, or double the value, when inorganic salts are employed. By 1888 the method of estimating the molecular weights based upon these observations was generally adopted, and consequently it was recognised, not only that the freezing point of a solution is related to the molecular weight of the dissolved substance, but that metallic salts produce an effect per molecule about twice as great as the effect produced by neutral carbon compounds such as sugar.

The presence of a substance dissolved in a liquid affects the other properties of the liquid, such as its viscosity, or, if volatile, its boiling point and the pressure of its vapour. The reduction of vapour pressure, and the raising of the boiling points of a number of liquids, have been subjects of repeated experiment during the last half-century; but the connection between the magnitude of the effect produced and the molecular weight of the dissolved substance was discovered so recently as 1887 by Raoult, whose work upon the freezing points of solutions has been already referred to. The law relating to vapour pressure has the same form as that which applies to freezing points; that is, the effect produced by molecular proportions of all substances in the same liquid is the same provided the solution is dilute. Hence the equation already given for the freezing point expresses the relation for the vapour pressure equally well, if we let A stand for the lowering of pressure produced by 1 gram of substance in 100 grams of solvent, and T for the effect produced by a molecular proportion of the substance in the same quantity of solvent.

The methods practically employed for estimating the effect of dissolving a definite quantity of substance in a volatile liquid, may be based upon the actual measurement of the pressure of the vapour of the solution when in a barometric vacuum, or upon the loss of weight sustained by a given quantity of the solution, as compared with the loss of weight of the same quantity of the pure solvent when a current of air is passed under the same conditions through both of them; or the method may be based upon observation of the boiling point at atmospheric pressure of the liquid before and after the dissolution in it of definite quantities of substance.

Again, if a solution of sugar or of a salt is separated from pure water by certain kinds of membrane, the volume of the solution increases by the entrance of water through the membrane, and a difference of pressure will be immediately established on the two sides of the membrane, which will go on increasing up to a certain maximum for each kind of dissolved substance. The pressure thus established is called the *osmotic pressure* of the dissolved substance. It appears to arise from the "semi-permeable" character of the membrane, which allows water to pass in either direction, but not the solute; hence water passes in the direction of the solution until the pressure it alone exerts per unit of surface is equal on both sides the septum, while on the side of the solution there is the additional pressure due to the solute. This can be measured and expressed in millimetres of mercury or otherwise. The cells of plant tissues are semi-permeable in this sense, and membranes formed by the precipitation of certain salts, especially cupric ferrocyanide within the pores of unglazed earthenware, have been used for the purpose of experiments on osmotic pressure. The earliest and best determinations of osmotic pressure, for which science is indebted to Professor W. Pfeffer the botanist,[1] have led to conclusions which stand in evident relation to the facts which have already been stated concerning the influence of dissolved substances on the properties of liquids, and they may be expressed nearly in the same terms. For it is found that the effect is again proportional to the strength of the solution, and when solutions of two distinct substances are compared, the osmotic pressure is found to be the same when each contains for 100 parts of the liquid *molecular proportions* of the dissolved substance.

In 1887 a theory was conceived which provided a beautiful explanation of all these various facts and relations. The first volume of the *Zeitschrift für physikalische Chemie* (pp. 481–508) contained a paper by Professor J. H. Van't Hoff which threw a flood

[1] "Osmotische Untersuchungen. Studien zur Zellenmechanik" (*Beiblätter*, ii., 1878, 182–193). See also Adie, *Trans. Chem. Soc.* 1891, 368.

of light upon the whole subject of solutions.[1] The theory, then for the first time brought forward, is based upon the recognition of the analogy between the state of substances in solution and the same in the state of gas. Pfeffer's results seem to have established the fact that osmotic pressure in dilute solutions is proportional to the amount of dissolved substance in unit mass, and that the pressure is directly proportional to the absolute temperature of the liquid. The laws of osmotic pressure, then, assume the same form as the law of Boyle, which connects pressure and volume, and the law of Gay-Lussac, which connects temperature and volume, for gases. And further, since molecular proportions of dissolved substances produce at the same temperature equal osmotic pressures, *equal volumes of different solutions*, which give the same osmotic pressures, *contain the same number of molecules.* This is equivalent to asserting that the law of Avogadro applies to solutions as well as to gases.

For the sake of clearness it may be as well, before proceeding further, to recall the main features and history of the kinetic theory of gases. From the phenomena of gaseous diffusion there seems to be very direct proof that the particles or molecules of gases are always moving about. This idea was long ago employed to explain their pressure and elasticity, but only in a general and rather indefinite way, and

[1] For an interesting summary of the course of events which led Van't Hoff to the theory, see *Berichte*, xxvii. (1894), 6.

it was in 1848 that Joule for the first time made some calculations as to the velocity which the particles of hydrogen and of oxygen must have in order to produce the observed pressure. He found that the particles of hydrogen, when at 0° C. and atmospheric pressure, move at the rate of more than 6000 feet per second, which is much faster than any ordinary projectile.[1]

A paper had been communicated to the Royal Society by J. J. Waterston in 1845, but unfortunately was not thought fit for publication at the time. Nearly half a century afterwards it was discovered by Lord Rayleigh in the archives of the Society, and was found to contain a nearly complete development of the theory which has since become so famous. This paper has been printed in the *Philosophical Transactions* for 1892. Views essentially the same as Waterston's were afterwards published by Krönig in 1856,[2] and by Clausius[3] in 1857.

The kinetic theory supposes that all the particles in a gas subsist in a state of perpetual movement with great velocity, but since they are very small, and much crowded together, no single molecule proceeds far in a straight line before it approaches another molecule, and its course is

[1] "On the Mechanical Equivalent of Heat, and on the Constitution of Elastic Fluids" (*Brit. Assoc. Rep.*, 1848, Pt. II. 21-22).
[2] "Grundzüge einer Theorie der Gase" (*Pogg. Ann.*, xcix. 315-322).
[3] "Ueber die Art der Bewegung welche wir Wärme nennen" (*Pogg. Ann.*, 1857, 353-380, and *Phil. Mag.*, xiv. 108-127).

altered, much in the same way that an elastic ball falling upon any surface rebounds and passes off in a new direction. The constitution of a liquid is supposed to be somewhat similar, the difference between a gas and a liquid being attributed to the association of a certain proportion of the moving molecules into groups; so that while in a true gas each molecule moves independently of the rest, except for collisions, in a liquid there is a mixture of free molecules and aggregations of molecules.

We may now return to the questions presented by the phenomena of electrolysis. It has already been stated that metallic salts generally, as well as acids and alkalis, when dissolved in a large quantity of water, cause a depression of the freezing point of the water nearly twice as great as the depression caused by the majority of carbon compounds. All these substances are electrolytes when in aqueous solution, while neutral carbon compounds are not. Now, by carrying the analogy between dilute solutions and the gaseous state a step further, an explanation is provided of the existence of these exceptions. This explanation is afforded by the doctrine of ionic dissociation introduced by Arrhenius in 1888. The abnormal vapour pressures of ammonium chloride, phosphoric chloride, sulphuric acid, and many other compounds are accounted for by the hypothesis that each molecule of such a compound when vaporised dissociates into two or more separate molecules, and in like manner the new theory supposes that substances which become electrolytes when dissolved owe the assumption of that character to a process of dissociation. The dissociation of sulphuric acid, for example, by the action of heat is, however, different in its cause as in its results, from the dissociation which is assumed to occur when it is mixed with water. Vapour of sulphuric acid is made up of equal numbers of molecules of water and sulphur trioxide, which, if cooled so that liquefaction occurs, unite together again, almost completely reproducing the original compound. Sulphuric acid diluted with water is supposed to yield a mixture of the ions H and SO_4, the number of molecules of the compound so resolved increasing in proportion to the dilution up to a limit.

A view which, at first sight, appears somewhat similar to this was proposed some forty years ago by Clausius,[1] almost immediately after his enunciation and discussion of the kinetic theory of gases. Clausius appears to have regarded a solution as consisting of a mixture of entire molecules moving about more or less rapidly, according to the temperature of the liquid, together with positive and negative partial molecules or ions, which owe their separation from one another to the encounters which result from the motion of heat. These partial molecules, moving irregularly through the liquid, meet

---

[1] R. Clausius, "Ueber die Elektricitätsleitung in Elektrolyten" (*Pogg.*, cL, 1857, 338; and *Phil. Mag.*, xv., 1858, 94).

now and then with complementary partial molecules, with which, when conditions are favourable, they reunite and reproduce the original compound, the number of free or ionised particles being, according to this view, dependent upon the temperature, increasing in numbers as the temperature is higher; while if the temperature is lowered the recombinations occur more frequently than the separations in unit time, so that, on the whole, there are fewer free ions in the liquid, while under no circumstances is it assumed that the number of partial molecules is more than a very small percentage of the number of entire molecules. A doctrine of the same kind had been enunciated by Williamson some years earlier in his memoir [1] on the "Theory of the Formation of Æther." The following passage explains his view quite clearly : "We are thus forced to admit that in an aggregate of molecules of any compound there is an exchange constantly going on between the elements which are contained in it. For instance, a drop of hydrochloric acid being supposed to be made up of a great number of molecules of the composition ClH, the proposition at which we have just arrived would lead us to believe that each atom of hydrogen does not remain quietly in juxtaposition with the atom of chlorine with which it first united, but on the contrary, is constantly changing places with other atoms of hydrogen, or, what is the same thing, changing chlorine.'

[1] *Phil. Mag.*, 1850.

Clausius, remarking upon this quotation, points out that Williamson's theory assumes a more frequent exchange of one atom for another than appears to him to be necessary for the explanation of electrolytic conduction, in which case he observes, "it is sufficient if the impact between complete molecules is occasionally and perhaps, comparatively speaking, rarely accompanied by an interchange of partial molecules."

Since these views were expressed by Clausius, facts have become known which seem to show that, if the comparison of the dissolved with the gaseous state is accepted, electrolytic conduction should depend upon and be proportional to a dissociated state in the dissolved electrolyte, which increases as solution is more dilute. It has been stated, for example, that the depression of the freezing point of a solution of such a neutral compound as sugar, a non-electrolyte, is only about half the depression observed in the solution of an acid or a metallic salt which is an electrolyte. Arrhenius[1] supposes that when an electrolyte is dissolved its ions separate from each other, not only, as assumed by Clausius, to a small extent, but to a large extent which increases with dilution; so that in an infinitely dilute solution none of the original molecules of the compound exist, but only the electrolytically active fragments of molecules or ions. When any electromotive force is applied to an electrolyte, therefore,

[1] *Zeitschr. Phys. Chem.*, i. (1887), 631.

the current which passes is proportional to the number of ions ready to convey the electricity.

There is therefore a fundamental difference between the earlier and the later views of the process of electrolysis. According to the well-known hypothesis of Grotthus, introduced in 1805, and to be found in all text-books of electricity to the present day, the molecules of an electrolyte upon which no electro-motive force is acting must be supposed to be distributed at random throughout the liquid, and to be arranged in no sort of order. When two metallic plates connected with a source of electricity are dipped into the liquid, say dilute sulphuric acid, the positive electricity of one plate attracts the oxygen, while the negative electricity of the other plate attracts the hydrogen, with the result that the molecules of acid range themselves in a multitude of polar chains across the space between the electrodes. Then, if the electro-motive force is sufficient, atoms of hydrogen are detached from one end of all these chains, while the residues of the molecules left take hydrogen from the adjoining molecules, and so the transfer of hydrogen from molecule to molecule occurs throughout each chain. Oxygen is liberated in a similar way at the surface of the opposite electrode, with a similar transfer of oxygen from molecule to molecule throughout the series of molecules forming each chain. And thus, while hydrogen and oxygen are liberated in visible bubbles at the surfaces of the electrodes, no action is perceptible within the liquid which fills the space between. A difficulty about this hypothesis, which has become apparent only within recent years, is that it assumes that the electrolyte is torn asunder into its ions by the action of the current. If that were the case, each chemical compound would require the application of a certain definite *minimum* electro-motive force peculiar to itself before electrolysis would begin. But decomposition occurs even when the electro-motive force is extremely weak, and it is therefore now more generally believed that the current does nothing more than direct to the respective electrodes the already separated ions. According to the Clausius hypothesis these are few at any one instant, but as fast as they are driven to the electrodes and are liberated, others are produced by dissociation within the liquid. According to the doctrine of Arrhenius, on the other hand, good electrolytic conductors are in a state of ionisation or dissociation, which is much more extensive, and which is increased by dilution up to a certain limit, when it may be nearly complete. The electric conductivity of a considerable number of electrolytes, including all the most important acids, has been determined chiefly by a method introduced by Kohlrausch, which is based on the employment of an alternating current, thus avoiding the difficulties arising from "polarisation" of the electrodes and other causes. The results of these experiments have led to the remarkable conclusion that electric conductivity is directly related to chemical activity. Thus the numbers expressing the electric conductivities of a series of acids of any given degree of dilution, also represent very closely the relative powers of the same acids to effect such chemical changes as the inversion of cane-sugar. The chemical activity of electrolytes is therefore directly related to the extent of the ionic dissociation of the substance, if we accept the hypothesis, and at the present time it must be admitted that there is no escape by way of any better explanation. The same hypothesis accords also with the well-known fact that many of the strongest acids, hydrogen chloride for example, are, when apart from water in the liquid state, both non-conductors and non-electrolytes, and at the same time almost destitute of chemical activity. The most characteristic of all the interactions produced by acids is that which follows from their contact with bases. This results in the general formation of salts and water, but an anomaly is here noticed which is almost inexplicable without the ionisation theory. The neutralisation of an acid by a base is attended by the evolution of heat, and it has been generally supposed that the amount of heat evolved in a given reaction is a measure of the activity of the affinities concerned, and of the amount of energy which escapes or runs down in the process. But when chemically equivalent quantities of different acids are neutralised by the same basic hydroxide, say soda NaHO, the amount of heat evolved by strong acids is not much greater than that afforded by acids reputed weak. Many experimental investigations of this subject have been undertaken, but the results of the work of Professor Julius Thomsen, of Copenhagen, may be regarded as the most exact and trustworthy. He found that when one molecule of soda, NaHO, dissolved in water is neutralised by different acids mixed with the same proportion of water, the amount of heat evolved may be represented by thermal units, expressed in the successive cases by the following numbers taken as examples:—

Name of acid.	Amount required by NaHO.	Heat evolved.
Hydrochloric acid	HCl	13740
Nitric acid	HNO_3	13617
Sulphuric acid	$\frac{1}{2}H_2SO_4$	15690
Phosphoric acid	$\frac{1}{3}H_3PO_4$	11343
Formic acid	$HCHO_2$	13450
Acetic acid	$HC_2H_3O_2$	13400

These examples suffice to show that the heat developed when an acid is neutralised by a basic hydroxide bears no very obvious relation to the chemical activity of the acid, as indicated by other chemical reactions in which it is capable of taking part. The ionisation hypothesis affords an explanation of this which is consistent with all the facts known. The heat produced in such changes as these is chiefly due to the formation of water, and not to the production of the several salts, which like the acids and bases are electrolytes, and are therefore, according to the hypothesis, dissociated to a considerable extent when in aqueous solution. The change which occurs when soda and hydrochloric acid are brought together is therefore not to be represented by the familiar equation—

$$HCl + NaHO = NaCl + H_2O.$$

The expression must take rather the following form :—
$$H + Cl + Na + HO = Na + Cl + H_2O.$$

And from this it appears that water is a compound which differs from caustic soda and nearly all other soluble oxides, chlorides, and salts, inasmuch as it is not under ordinary circumstances ionised to any appreciable extent. This agrees with what is known of the properties of water as an electrolyte. It results from the experiments of Davy, and all who have followed since his time, that water is a very bad conductor, and its conductivity diminishes in proportion as it is deprived of dissolved salts or other substances. Pure water is very difficult to make, and still more difficult to preserve; but when every precaution has been taken to avoid contamination from the vessel in which it is kept, and from the atmosphere surrounding it, the conductivity is so small that it has never been determined with accuracy. It is perhaps owing to this remarkable peculiarity that water so well plays its part in nature as a liquid which is almost absolutely neutral, and save as a solvent usually exhibits very little chemical activity.

The heat of neutralisation of acids per equivalent is from 13,000 to 14,000 calories on the average. The differences noticeable in the values given above are attributed to the different extent of ionisation in the different acids when mixed with the same amounts of water. They are also partly due to the fact that in some cases, notably that of phosphoric acid, the normal sodium salt supposed to be formed is partially decomposed in the presence of water into soda and acid, and hence the interaction between equivalent quantities of base and acid is in such cases incomplete.

Such in broad outline are the views accepted by, we must suppose, the majority of chemists at the present day. They are consistent enough among themselves, but while they help to connect together many facts and phenomena they are still attended by many difficulties, and leave much that has always been obscure still unexplained.

The ions, according to Arrhenius, are associated with electric charges, but whence these charges are derived is far from intelligible. Taking common salt, for example, this substance in the solid state is universally supposed to be made up of atoms of sodium in juxtaposition with atoms of chlorine; when the salt is dissolved in water a large proportion of the whole number of molecules are at once resolved into ions of sodium with a positive charge, and ions of chlorine with an equal negative charge, and if the liquid is diluted the number of these dissociated and charged particles increases till there are very few, if any, molecules of salt left. It does not appear necessary to the ionic doctrine, however, to assume the permanent residence of charges of electricity upon the separated atoms. It is only necessary to state what is the fact, that there are two classes of elementary atoms. One of these includes hydrogen and the metals which, in virtue of some peculiarity of their structure, are capable of becoming associated with a unit charge of positive electricity, and conveying this from the positive electrode to the negative in the process of electrolysis. The other class includes oxygen, the halogens, sulphur, and perhaps some others, which are similarly endowed with the power of conveying negative electricity only, and in the process of electrolysis travel with their unit charges from the negative to the positive surface. On such a hypothesis the initial difficulty as to the determining cause of ionisation when a substance like salt is dissolved in water, is certainly not greater than that which attends the ordinary view; and, further, it may be pointed out that it is not yet proved that all the elements come within the two classes just mentioned. Carbon notably seems to be incapable of assuming the ionic state. Its chlorides are non-electrolytes, as are all its hydrides, and when electrolysis of a compound of carbon like acetic acid occurs, the hydrogen ion goes to the cathode as usual, while the carbon, carrying also some hydrogen with it, accompanies the oxygen to the cathode. The old question is, in fact, not yet finally answered: is chemical combination due to the joining together of electrically charged atoms? in other words, is "chemical affinity" identical with electricity? This may be true of acids, bases, and salts, but there is nothing to lead us to suspect that the atoms of carbon, hydrogen, and oxygen in sugar are held together in any such way. If the chemical energy of the sodium and chlorine becomes electrical when common salt dissolves, there is no obvious reason why the chemical energy of the sugar should not, at least in part, undergo a corresponding change, and give an electrolyte, of which the hydroxyl present in the sugar molecule would naturally be the negative ion. Sugar, however, shows a normal osmotic pressure, and does not conduct electrolytically. It seems improbable that the complex molecules formed by carbon compounds, in which are frequently concerned forty or fifty atoms of carbon, perhaps twice that number of atoms of hydrogen and oxygen, beside nitrogen, are held together by the operation of any agency which requires *opposition of quality*, a positive and a negative, in juxtaposition to account for the union of any two atoms together.

The only compounds of carbon which are capable of pure electrolytic decomposition are those which play the part of acids, and in such cases the carbonyl group, CO.OH, is usually present, and is resolved into H, which goes to the cathode, while the CO.O passes to the anode, dragging with it all the remaining carbon, hydrogen, and other atoms which are attached to it in the compound. It is easy enough to see why the conductivity of trichloracetic acid, $CCl_3.COOH$, so greatly exceeds that of acetic acid, for the anion has not the burden of hydrogen atoms to carry to the electrode, but has in the chlorine a passenger which actually helps to row the boat across.

Nitrogen is another element about the capability of which to form an ion there is some room for doubt. Ammonia is not an electrolyte unless dissolved in water, and then it behaves as a hydroxide. Nitric acid is resolved into H and NO_3, which is further broken up by electrolysis. The only compound in which nitrogen alone figures as an ion appears to be the remarkable hydrazoic acid, or diazo-imide, of which the ions must be H and N_3. This seems to deserve some further investigation.

In 1880 Professor H. B. Dixon[1] discovered the remarkable fact that a mixture of carbonic oxide and oxygen completely dried is not inflamed by the passage of an electric spark in contact with the gas. This attracted attention to other facts previously known, which seemed to prove that chlorine in the absence of moisture was very far from being the active substance commonly supposed. Chlorine, it is now known, may be kept in contact with

[1] *Brit. Assoc. Report* (1880), 503.

sodium, or with copper, for years without tarnishing the lustre of the metal, provided both have been most carefully dried, while on the introduction of a drop of water instantaneous combination occurs. Other experiments by W. H. Brereton Baker have demonstrated that the combustion of carbon, sulphur, and even phosphorus in oxygen is prevented at temperatures considerably above the ordinary igniting points of these substances if moisture is removed as completely as possible,[1] and that even ammonia and hydrogen chloride,[2] and nitric oxide and oxygen do not combine when both gases are perfectly dry. On these and some other results attempts have been made to construct a new electro-chemical theory of combination, which, however, requires that in *all* cases of union a small quantity of some third substance, not necessarily water, must be present. Facts, however, are at present in opposition to the general application of such a view, and it will be necessary to study the conditions of chemical change yet more fully and completely before anything more than partial and tentative hypothesis will be within reach.

[1] *Proc. Roy. Soc.*, xlv. 1–3.
[2] *Trans. Chem. Soc.* (1894), 611–624.

CHAPTER IX

DISCOVERIES RELATING TO THE LIQUEFACTION OF GASES

It is perhaps not surprising that the older chemists, down to the middle of the seventeenth century, should have been almost entirely ignorant as to the relation of "volatile spirits" and air to other kinds of matter, and that no clear distinctions could be drawn between the different kinds of air, whether as to chemical composition or physical properties, till the experiments of Black, Priestley, Cavendish, and Lavoisier in the middle of the eighteenth century brought so much new light upon this difficult subject. For, down to our own day, notwithstanding exact knowledge as to their composition, a purely arbitrary distinction prevailed between "permanent" gases and other kinds of vaporisable substance. We owe the abolition of this artificial and baseless distinction, and our present convictions as to the unity of the essential nature of all terrestrial matter, to a long course of experimental inquiry, the history of which during these later years forms a tangled web, the several threads of which are very difficult to follow clearly, and the pursuit of which would not be very profitable to the student.[1]

The first recorded reference to the liquefaction of a commonly recognised gas occurs in "Fourcroy's Chemistry," vol. ii. p. 74, where it is stated, without any description of the process, that Citizens Monge and Clouet have liquefied sulphurous acid (sulphur dioxide). The next experiment of the same kind was made by Northmore, who, in 1805, reduced chlorine and probably also sulphurous acid to the liquid state by compressing the gas, by means of a brass condensing syringe, into a pear-shaped glass receiver.[2] From this time till the subject was taken up by Faraday no gases were reduced to liquid, but in the interval Cagniard de la Tour carried out his remarkable investigation into the action of heat upon volatile liquids.[3] By heating to various temperatures water, or ether, or alcohol, contained in a gun-barrel stopped at each end, he was able to prove that such liquid may be wholly changed into vapour, notwithstanding the existence of an enormous pressure, and in the case of ether the vapour thus formed occupies a volume less than twice the volume of the liquid from which it is produced. By enclosing a stone ball in the tube along with the

---

[1] A tolerably complete and impartial statement of the contributions made to the subject of the liquefaction of gases by various experimenters who have devoted themselves to it, is given by Prince Kropotkin in the *Nineteenth Century* for Aug. 1898.

[2] *Nicholson's Journal*, xii. and xiii.

[3] *Ann. Chim.*, 2nd series, xxi. 127, 178, and xxii. 410.

liquid, he was able to tell when the liquid had entirely evaporated by the character of the sound produced within by rolling the ball to and fro, and he even succeeded in making some rough estimations of the pressure of the vapour within. Similar results were afterwards obtained in glass tubes.

The researches which ultimately led to the liquefaction of all known gases were begun by Faraday and Davy in 1823. The example of steam, which is known to be condensable to liquid water either by cooling or by pressure, would lead naturally to the belief that some at least of the substances called gases might be vapours of very volatile liquids condensable like steam to liquid. In dealing with a gas two methods present themselves when the object is to subject it to pressure: the one already used by Northmore consists in the direct application of mechanical pressure by means of a pump; the other consists in enclosing materials from which the gas can be generated within a tube strong enough to resist the pressure of the gas as it accumulates. The latter was the method used by Faraday. The first case examined was that of chlorine, which had been found by Faraday himself to form a crystalline compound with water. It is now a little doubtful what idea led to the heating of these crystals in a closed tube, and whether it occurred first to Davy or to his assistant. Faraday had been previously occupied with chlorine, and had discovered two chlorides of carbon in 1820. But Davy seems to have suggested the experiment which led to the observation of liquid chlorine, and to have regarded the condensation of the gases as his own subject (see Faraday's "Researches," p. 139). Immediately after this muriatic acid was liquefied by a similar method, in which the materials used were sal-ammoniac and sulphuric acid, and Faraday, there can be no doubt, was the operator. Faraday also liquefied in glass tubes sulphurous acid, sulphuretted hydrogen, carbonic acid, nitrous oxide, euchlorine, cyanogen, and ammonia. There then remained only the gases of the atmosphere, namely, oxygen and nitrogen, beside hydrogen, marsh gas, carbonic oxide, and nitric oxide, which resisted all attempts by this method to change their state, and arsenetted hydrogen, hydriodic and hydrobromic acids, which were easily overcome by Faraday when some twenty years later he resumed his experiments upon the subject. In the meantime Thilorier in Paris, acting upon the same principle, with the substitution of metallic cylinders for glass tubes, prepared large quantities of liquid carbonic acid, and was the first to obtain this substance in a solid state.[1] For this purpose he used the now familiar method of allowing a jet of the liquid to escape through a fine orifice into a box of peculiar construction, where, in consequence of the evaporation of a portion of the liquid, the rest is chilled below its freezing point, and accumulates in the form of a fine snow-like

[1] *Ann. Chim.*, lx. (1835), 432.

powder. This solid material has ever since played a prominent part in many experiments requiring a low temperature, and though it is not by the aid of solid carbon dioxide that the most remarkable results have been obtained, it remains to this day an extremely valuable cryogenic agent. In 1845 Faraday published[1] the results of further attempts to liquefy the gases remaining unsubdued by his earlier method. He now employed two pumps for compression, and glass tubes fitted with stop-cocks as receivers. The latter he cooled to a temperature of 166° F. below zero, by means of solid carbonic acid and ether boiling under reduced pressure. In stating the considerations which led him to employ this agent, and in discussing the want of success in dealing with the six so-called permanent gases, Faraday evidently had ideas which came very near to an anticipation of the important principle established twenty years later by Andrews. With regard to the experimental conditions he says, "As my hopes of success, beyond that heretofore obtained, depended more upon depression of temperature than on the pressure which I could employ in these tubes, I endeavoured to obtain a still greater degree of cold. There are, in fact, some results producible by cold which no pressure may be able to effect. Again, that beautiful condition which Cagniard de la Tour has made known, and which comes on with liquids at a certain heat, may have its point of temperature for some of

[1] *Phil. Trans.* (1845), 155, and "Collected Works," p. 96.

the bodies to be experimented with, as oxygen, hydrogen, nitrogen, &c., below that belonging to the bath of carbonic acid and ether; and in that case no pressure which any apparatus could bear would be able to bring them into the liquid or solid state." And later on he observes that "the temperature of $-166°$ F. below $0°$, low as it is, is probably *above* this point of temperature for hydrogen, and perhaps oxygen and nitrogen; and then no compression, without the conjoint application of a degree of cold below that we have as yet obtained, can be expected to take from them their gaseous state."

Here, then, the resources of the physical laboratory seemed to have been exhausted, and it is probable that, slowly as successive steps toward the desired end, the reduction of the remaining intractable gases, seemed to be accomplished, progress would have been still further delayed but for the important experiments of Andrews, which, though carried on during many years, were not published *in extenso* till 1869.[1] Previously to 1863 Dr. Andrews had observed that "on partially liquefying carbonic acid by pressure alone, and gradually raising at the same time the temperature to $88°$ F., the surface of demarcation between the liquid and gas became fainter, lost its curvature, and at last disappeared. The space was then occupied by a homogeneous fluid, which exhibited, when the

---

[1] "On the Continuity of the Gaseous and Liquid States of Matter:" The Bakerian Lecture (*Phil. Trans.*, 1869, ii. 575).

pressure was suddenly diminished or the temperature slightly lowered, a peculiar appearance of moving or flickering striæ throughout its entire mass. At temperatures above 88° no apparent liquefaction [1] of carbonic acid, or separation into two distinct forms of matter, could be effected even when a pressure of 300 or 400 atmospheres was applied." Andrews then proceeded to make a series of exact comparisons of the volume assumed by carbonic acid and air when submitted to pressure at successive degrees of temperatures starting from that of the air. The results are most easily intelligible with the aid of the diagram given in the Bakerian Lecture. Here the curves are drawn with reference to two axes of rectangular co-ordinates; the volumes occupied by the gases being the ordinates, and the pressures the abscissæ, while the temperatures marked on each curve are maintained constant.

The difference in the behaviour of carbonic acid and air when submitted to gradually increasing pressure at the temperature of the air is well shown by the curves. While air is steadily reduced in volume as pressure increases, from 1 up to 110 atmospheres, carbonic acid contracts at all temperatures more rapidly than would be indicated by Boyle's law, and at the pressure of 49·89 atmospheres liquefaction begins. This is shown in the

---

[1] It is interesting here to compare Faraday's remark in 1845: "I am inclined to think that at 90° Cagniard de la Tour's state comes on with carbonic acid."—*Collected Works*, p. 109.

curve marked 13°·1 by the sudden change from a slope to a vertical direction. The other curves show the nature of the volume changes which ensue when the same increase of pressure is applied at higher temperatures. Above 30°·92 C. or 87°·7 F. Andrews found that no pressure was capable of producing visible liquefaction. This temperature,

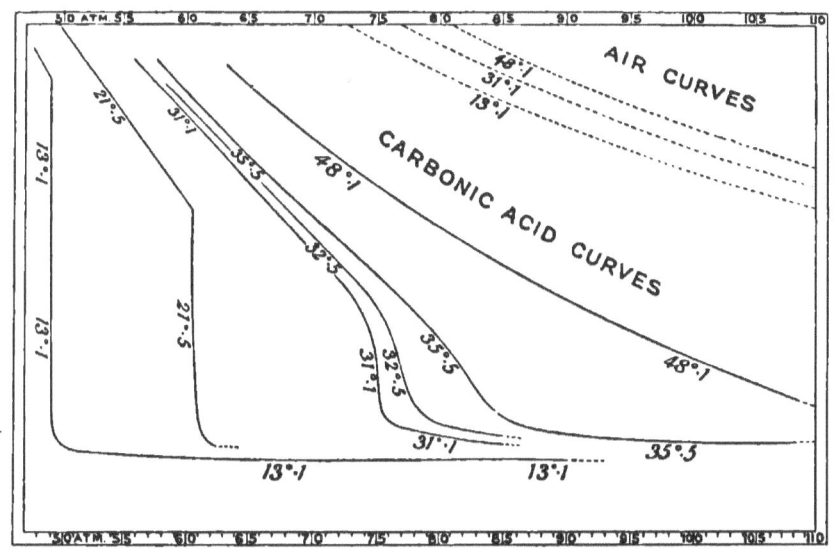

then, is called the critical point; below this liquefaction occurs when sufficient pressure is applied, above it carbonic acid behaves more nearly like a permanent gas in proportion as the temperature is raised. All other gases behave in a similar way.

On this series of observations Andrews was able to base an interesting distinction between a "gas" and a "vapour," terms which up to this time had been used in an uncertain and arbitrary way. "Ether," he says, "in the state of gas is called a vapour, while sulphurous acid in the same state is called a gas; yet they are both vapours, the one derived from a liquid boiling at 35°, the other from a liquid boiling at $-10°$. . . . Many of the properties of vapours depend on the gas and liquid being present in contact with one another, and this we have seen can only occur at temperatures below the critical point. We may accordingly define a vapour to be a gas at any temperature under its critical point. . . . If this definition be accepted, carbonic acid will be a vapour below 31°, a gas above that temperature; ether a vapour below 200°, a gas above that temperature."

The most important deduction from the results of these experiments, then, supplies a clear explanation of the difficulty encountered in attempting the liquefaction of the six exceptional gases. Up to this time the lowest temperatures attainable had been above the critical points of all of them. It is now known that the critical temperature of oxygen, for example, is about $-118°\cdot 8$C., and that of nitrogen $-146°\cdot$ C. It was not till towards the close of the year 1877, that two experimenters working along distinct lines arrived by the use of two different methods at substantially the same result. On the 24th December 1877, at the meeting of the French Academy, two communications announcing the liquefaction of oxygen were received, the one from M. Raoul Pictet of Geneva, the other from M. Louis Cailletet[1] of Chatillon-sur-Seine. Pictet[2] employed what was essentially the method of Faraday, that is, he generated the gas within a closed vessel, where by its accumulation pressure was generated, and he cooled the tube containing the gas. He attained the success which was denied to Faraday, by the more efficient cooling of the gas. By means of the evaporation of liquid sulphur dioxide, the temperature of $-65°$ C. is reached, and at this point carbon dioxide is easily liquefied. By the rapid boiling of the liquid thus produced, the temperature of $-140°$ C. is attained. This is below the critical point for oxygen, and the pressure employed by Pictet in his first experiments, amounting to about 475 atmospheres, was, therefore, excessive and unnecessary. Liquid oxygen was formed in considerable quantity, but the announcement in the following month of the liquefaction and solidification of hydrogen was evidently based upon some error of observation, for we now know that the critical temperature of hydrogen is nearly $120°$ lower in the scale.

Cailletet employed an apparatus, ever since familiarly known as a laboratory appliance under the name of the Cailletet pump, whereby a gas

[1] "De la condensation de l'oxygène et de l'oxyde de carbone," L. Cailletet (*Compt. Rend.*, lxxxv. 1213).

[2] "Expériences sur la liquéfaction de l'oxygène." R. Pictet (*Compt. Rend.*, lxxxv. 1214).

can be submitted to considerable pressure, and when greatly reduced in volume the pressure can be suddenly relieved. Under these conditions the expansion of the gas produces cooling, in consequence of which a portion of it appears in the form of minute droplets, of which a part remains suspended in the gas, giving the appearance of a cloud, and part usually collects in visible streams upon the side of the tube containing it. With this apparatus Cailletet reduced to the liquid state oxygen and carbonic oxide, beside ethylene and acetylene, marsh gas and nitric oxide.

Two now remained of the original six uncondensable gases, namely, nitrogen and hydrogen. Nitrogen yielded in 1883, in the hands of the Polish Professors Wroblewski and Olszewski[1]; but hydrogen resisted for many years the almost continuous efforts which were made to collect it in the liquid form, though in 1884 Wroblewski[2] announced that he had observed an appearance of ebullition as of liquid in the gas under experiment. This was contradicted by Olszewski, who in his turn almost immediately afterwards[3] declared that he had obtained a similar effect under somewhat different conditions. The difficulties of the investigation now increased enormously, and it is not surprising that progress was slow, considering both the great pecuniary cost of the work, involving as it

[1] *Compt. Rend.*, xcvi. 1140 and 1225.
[2] Ibid., xcviii. 304. [3] Ibid., xcviii. 365.

did the construction of much expensive apparatus, and the use of large quantities of liquefied gases, as well as the considerable personal risk involved in the employment of the very high pressures which the various reservoirs of gas were required to sustain. Henceforward, for nearly twenty years no new principle was introduced. Cailletet in 1882 recommended the use of liquid ethylene for the production of low temperatures, and when by the aid of ethylene oxygen in a liquid state could be obtained in fairly large quantity, this also was employed as a refrigerant. The application of external cold to the vessel containing the highly compressed gas was also associated with the cooling effect produced by expansion as in Cailletet's method, and it was in this way that nitrogen was first liquefied by Wroblewski and Olszewski in 1883, as already mentioned. By a similar process Olszewski got evidence of the liquefaction of hydrogen, and was able a few years later to determine its critical temperature and boiling point[1] with some considerable approach to accuracy.

About this time, namely, in 1884, the production of low temperatures and the liquefaction of gases became a subject of research in the laboratory of the Royal Institution, under Professor Dewar. He, like the Russian chemists, employed liquid nitrous oxide and ethylene as cooling agents, but save in the dimensions of the apparatus, no essential differ-

[1] *Phil. Mag.*, Aug. 1895.

ence is apparent in the published accounts of the methods of procedure, the principles involved being exactly the same. The collection of large quantities of liquid oxygen and liquid air has, however, provided the means of producing and maintaining a low temperature for a length of time, sufficient to allow a number of important investigations to be carried on, which have resulted in the discovery of many interesting facts relating to the physical and chemical properties of matter at temperatures not far above the absolute zero. Some of these will be referred to later on.

In the course of this work an ingenious device of Professor Dewar's has provided the means of avoiding one serious difficulty. Of course all objects at the common temperature of a room are at some 200 degrees Centigrade above the boiling points of these very volatile liquids, and hence any glass or other vessel used for their collection is relatively very hot. When the liquid is poured into such a vessel violent boiling at first occurs until the temperature of the glass is reduced to that of the liquid. But even then heat passes from the air into the walls of the vessel, and so to the liquid, fast enough to cause very rapid evaporation and loss. This is avoided by immersing the vessel in which the liquid is to be collected in a second vessel, also of glass, united with it at the mouth, and completely removing the air from the space between the two. Across such a vacuous space no heat can be brought by convection of air, and as under ordinary circumstances the amount of heat which is radiated to the contents of such a jacketed receiver is relatively small, vessels of this kind afford the means of storing liquid air, or oxygen, even for hours, while the rate of evaporation becomes exceedingly slow.

The year 1895 will be memorable for the introduction of a principle which, though previously known, had never before been made the basis of a method for effecting the cooling of a compressed gas. It has, of course, long been known that when a gas is compressed it becomes heated, and if the operation is performed quickly, so that there is no time for much loss by radiation or conduction, the temperature may be raised very considerably. This is often demonstrated by the use of the so-called "fire syringe," which consists of a strong glass tube closed at one end and fitted with a piston. By introducing a drop of an inflammable liquid, such as ether or carbon bisulphide, and then suddenly forcing down the piston, so as to squeeze the air into a relatively small volume, a flash of light is seen, which is produced by the ignition of the mixed air and vapour in the tube. Supposing a quantity of air compressed by a piston in a similar manner, and the heat disengaged is allowed to pass away, upon allowing the gas to expand again, and so to lift the piston against the pressure of the atmosphere, a corresponding cooling effect will result, and the temperature of the air will be lowered. This is, in fact, the principle made use of in the most ordinary refrigerating machines, which are used for making ice for preserving meat, and for other purposes.

About 1844 Joule made a number of experiments upon this subject, and demonstrated that the cold produced by the dilatation of a gas results from the conversion of heat into work in accordance with the universal principle. He thought at first that if the dilatation was so arranged that the gas did no work, then no cooling would result. But it was pointed out later by Professor W. Thomson[1] (now Lord Kelvin), that this is only approximately true for ordinary gases, which do not strictly comply with the gaseous laws connecting volume with pressure and temperature, and that some cooling would occur under such conditions, the effect being the greater in gases which, like carbonic acid gas, were less perfect than others, like air. This was verified by experiment, gases under considerable pressure being allowed to escape through a porous plug. Air at 16° C. was found to be reduced in temperature about ·26 of a degree Centigrade for each atmosphere of release, oxygen at 0° was cooled ·316° C., and carbon dioxide 1·252° C. per atmosphere. The amount of such cooling is approximately inversely as the square of the absolute temperature, so that the colder the gas is while under pressure the more it is cooled by release. At about $-130°$ C. com-

---

[1] Thomson's "Mathematical and Physical Papers," vol. i. ("Thermal Effects of Fluids").

pressed air is cooled to the extent of about 1° per atmosphere taken off.

This principle has been applied not only by Cailletet in the apparatus successfully used in the liquefaction of oxygen, but by later workers in the various attempts to reduce hydrogen to the liquid state. Thus Olszewski, in 1884, exposed hydrogen gas under a pressure of about 150 atmospheres to the temperature of $-211°$ by means of liquid oxygen boiling under reduced pressure. The pressure of the hydrogen was then reduced to about 20 atmospheres, and being thus reduced in temperature below its critical point a portion of it was liquefied.

Siemens, in 1857, seems to have had the idea of "regenerating" cold by applying the same principle which is used in his well-known regenerative furnace for the storage of heat, but this idea was never carried into practice. Later, in 1885, Solvay patented a process based upon the same principle, which involved the use of an expansion cylinder. By such methods, however, the difficulty of excluding access of heat from without puts a rather narrow limit upon the amount of cooling actually attainable.

More recently a method has been devised by which such cooling effect can be made practically cumulative, the gas while still under pressure being cooled by another portion of the same immediately after release. A description of such apparatus by which practical results upon a large scale were obtainable was given for the first time by Herr Linde, an engineer, of Munich;[1] but a patent for an application of the same principle had been obtained previously (May 23, 1895) in England by Dr. W. Hampson. Both machines have since undergone modification in detail, and are now employed successfully on a manufacturing scale for the liquefaction of air for use as a refrigerating agent, and for other purposes. It is impossible to describe the apparatus in detail without the use of many diagrams, but from what has already been said it will be easily anticipated that it is only necessary to provide a spiral copper tube having a fine hole at its extremity for the escape of the compressed gas, and a metal cylinder surrounding the coil through which the gas enters, so that the gas cooled by expansion is made to return over the coils of pipe before escaping into the air. The entering gas thus has its temperature continuously brought lower and lower, till at last it is reduced below the critical point of the gas, and the pressure being sufficient a portion of the gas liquefies, and is blown in drops and spray out of the hole at the end of the spiral. Of course the whole arrangement requires to be very efficiently protected by non-conducting material against the entrance of heat from the outside air.

By such means, then, all those substances formerly spoken of as "permanent" gases have been seen in

[1] An account of these experiments was given in the *Engineer*, Oct. 4, 1895; and later more fully in the Howard Lectures, by Professor Ewing (*Journal of the Society of Arts*, 1897, p. 1091).

the liquid state, and most of them also in the form of solids. Nevertheless hydrogen alone remained unobtainable in quantity to allow of its more complete study. The boiling point and critical temperature were known approximately from the experiments of Olszewski, but all attempts had failed to liquefy the element in such quantity that it could be retained in an open vessel under atmospheric pressure. This important and interesting result has now been achieved in the laboratory of the Royal Institution under the direction of Professor Dewar. The apparatus employed has not been described in detail, but it is understood to be constructed upon the principle already indicated of cumulative cooling by expansion from pressure. The difficulties to be overcome were unquestionably very great, and success could only be hoped for in the hands of an operator prepared for the task by years of experience in the management of the complicated machinery necessary in work of the kind. It is both interesting and gratifying that the final victory which crowns the long series of successful attacks upon the apparently impregnable position of the permanent gases should have been recorded in the laboratory of the Royal Institution, where the first successes in this field were won by Faraday. The facts are as follows:—

On May 10, 1898, hydrogen was for the first time seen to drop from the nozzle of the apparatus into a specially constructed receiver, where some

20 cubic centimetres, or nearly three-quarters of a fluid ounce, collected in about five minutes. Larger quantities have since been obtained, but the proportion of the whole gas reduced to the liquid state is only about 1 per cent. Hydrogen in the liquid state is a clear, colourless liquid which exhibits a well-defined surface. It is remarkable for its low density. This was determined by measuring the volume of the gas obtained by evaporating 10 cubic centimetres, and was found to be rather less than 0·07, or about *one-fourteenth the density of liquid water* at 0°. One interesting point as to the relations of hydrogen seems to have been settled by these results. The favourite idea, probably originating with Graham, and generally held for many years, has been that hydrogen was the vapour of a very volatile metal. Its association with the metals in chemical and electrolytic decompositions, and the absorption of large quantities of the gas by palladium without loss of its metallic properties, always seemed to be consistent with this notion. But it is now clear that hydrogen in the liquid state does not exhibit the characteristics of a metal, but seems rather to find its nearest analogues in the gases of the paraffin series, marsh gas and the rest, though liquid hydrogen has only about one sixth the density of liquid marsh gas.

The boiling point of this wonderful liquid was found to be about 238° below the Centigrade zero, and therefore about 35° above the hypothetical absolute zero. The question so often debated as to what would happen if a gas could be cooled to this absolute zero is already partly answered. All gases change to liquids before the zero is reached, and now what would ensue if the liquid could be deprived completely of heat seemed within the possibility of settlement. We know that when a liquid is made to boil it carries off heat—so-called latent heat—in the resulting vapour, and if changed into vapour by reduction of pressure only, the latent heat is supplied at the expense of its own sensible heat, and cooling is the result. Professor Dewar has, of course, lost no time in making an experiment of this kind with liquid hydrogen. The result, however, was disappointing.

Under a pressure equal to about 25 millimetres of mercury the liquid hydrogen evaporated quietly and steadily, remaining clear and colourless to the eye; but the temperature fell only about one degree below the boiling point under atmospheric pressure, whereas it was expected that it would have been some ten degrees lower. In such cases, of course, all ordinary thermometers are useless, and temperatures have to be determined by a platinum resistance coil. It is possible that the thermometer is at fault in this case, but the cause of this unexpected result is not at present known. It seems likely, however, that the absolute zero of the thermometric scale will remain for some time a subject upon which the scientific imagination can continue to be exercised,

R

CHAPTER X

SUMMARY AND CONCLUSION

It must now be evident to the reader that ideas of the present day relating to the act of chemical combination and the nature and constitution of chemical compounds are very different from those of a hundred or even fifty years ago. The Atomic Theory has been not only received as affording a plausible explanation of the familiar quantitative laws of chemical combination, but the theory has been enthroned as the predominant and indispensable doctrine to which every question in modern chemistry is referred, and of which the triumphs of modern theory supply the justification. Without the Atomic Theory and the doctrine of the orderly linking of atoms, the natural outcome of the recognition of that property of atoms which is now called their valency, " organic " chemistry would be a heap of confusion, and progress very slow if not impossible. The Atomic Theory, however, was not established without a struggle. The early crude results of quantitative analysis were sufficient for the genius of Dalton; but the fixity of combining proportions can hardly be said to have been fully established till the researches of Stas (p. 77) supplied the necessary facts. The problem which led Berthollet in the early years of the century to dispute the truth of this fundamental proposition is one which has ever since afforded material both for experimental inquiry and theoretical discussion. We are quite satisfied now that every chemical compound is definite in its nature, and that its constituents are joined together in proportions which cannot be varied except *per saltum*, and then a new substance is produced. But the youngest student in practical chemistry soon finds out that the production of any given compound is largely dependent upon the conditions of the experiment. Of these conditions, one very important is the relation between the quantities of the acting materials, another is the nature of the products of their interaction, whether solid, liquid, or gaseous, soluble or not soluble in the menstruum employed, and so forth. A beautiful experiment, illustrating the effect of mass or relative quantity, may be seen by mixing together a dilute solution of ferric chloride in water with a similar solution of potassium thiocyanate, when the familiar red coloration due to the production of ferric thiocyanate appears. If now this liquid be divided into two equal parts, and to one is added some more of the ferric chloride, a deepening of tint will be observed, which seems to indicate that the iron was deficient in the original mixture. But if to the other portion of the red solution a further dose of the thiocyanate is added, a similar deepening at once results. This, on the other hand, seems to show that the thiocyanate was added to the original in insufficient amount. These results seem contradictory, and at first sight the explanation is not apparent; but on trial it will be found that, in order to produce the maximum effect, one or the other of the acting materials must be used in very great excess over and above the quantity indicated by the theoretical equation which would be used to express the change. And so in many other instances we have to seek the conditions under which, in any system of bodies capable of acting upon one another, equilibrium can be established. In most of these cases the changes which occur are reversible; that is, they proceed in one direction till certain quantities of the products of interaction have accumulated, and the action then comes to an end. This we can now explain by a hypothesis which in its original form we owe to Williamson (see p. 226). It is now clear that we must exchange the older statical views of chemical compounds, and their modes of interaction with other compounds, for others which involve the idea of motion among the atoms.

In every such system as that described above we have two changes going on simultaneously, the one between the two original substances, in this case ferric chloride and potassium thiocyanate, and the other between the products of their interaction, namely, potassium chloride and ferric thiocyanate. If these two changes take place at different rates, more and more of one of these pairs of compounds will accumulate; when they go on at the same rate, then action appears to be at an end, because equilibrium has been established. The action, however, must be supposed to continue, and the equilibrium results from the two opposite interactions proceeding at the same rate. Such changes are generally represented by an equation in which the sign of equality is replaced by a pair of arrows pointing in opposite directions, to signify that the equation may be read backwards or forwards, thus:—

$$FeCl_3 + 3KCNS \rightleftarrows Fe(CNS)_3 + 3KCl.$$

If now into such a system in equilibrium a larger quantity of any one of the substances present is introduced, a disturbance is set up which leads to the redistribution of its elements to a greater or less extent. This disturbance, there is reason to believe, is dependent upon the increased opportunities which are afforded to the constituents of the added substance of meeting and reacting with the other elements present; in the case taken by way of illustration, the addition of more of the iron salt gives increased chances for the iron to find out the unchanged thiocyanate present in the liquid, and *vice versâ*. Of course, in all such cases the extent of the change is also largely dependent upon temperature, and where gaseous products are formed it is also much dependent upon pressure. The nature of the solvent employed is important, for in the event of gas escaping, or of a solid precipitating, a part of the material is eliminated from the sphere of action, and a disturbance of proportions ensues. In such cases the theoretically possible change is usually completely accomplished.

So early as 1852 experiments were made by Bunsen,[1] with the object of testing the "Law of Mass." He exploded mixtures of hydrogen and carbonic oxide with oxygen in different proportions, insufficient to burn both the gases; but the conclusions he arrived at were afterwards shown to be erroneous.

Studies relating to the rate at which chemical change proceeds in particular cases have been undertaken by many chemists during the last forty years. One of the earliest was the investigation of the formation of compound ethers, by the interaction of alcohol with acids, by Berthelot.[1] He found, as we should now expect, that the interaction proceeds more and more slowly as the ether and water are formed, until ultimately it comes to an end, although both acid and alcohol remain in the liquid. Another important research was carried out by A. Vernon Harcourt and W. Esson,[2] in which they demonstrated the influence upon the rate of change of varying the proportions of the materials in the

---

[1] *Ann. Chim. Phys.*, 1862 [3], lxv. 385; lxvi. 110.
[2] *Jour. Chem. Soc.*, 1867, v. 459.

reactions they examined. Other special cases have been examined by Gladstone, Horstmann, Dixon, Deville, Ostwald, Thomsen, and others, some of whom have been referred to in a previous chapter. But the merit of formulating the fundamental principle of the action of mass, and thus bringing into scientific form previous vague notions about affinity, belongs to the Norwegian physicists Guldberg and Waage. Their book, entitled *Études sur les affinités chimiques*, published by the University of Christiania in 1867, contains an investigation of the law of mass action, which has been of great service to theoretical chemistry. A discussion of the theorem would be unsuitable to these pages, but sufficient has been said to indicate the general nature of the inquiry.

Temperature, as already explained, is a very important factor in the circumstances which determine the rate of chemical change. At the low temperatures now obtainable by liquid air or oxygen all chemical activity seems to be suspended, while at the opposite end of the scale, at the temperatures of the electric arc or spark, all ordinary chemical compounds seem to be broken up into their elements.

Chemical combination, then, is an affair of atoms, and their joining together or separating is regulated by "affinity," by temperature and pressure, and by the mass or relative quantities of the materials presented to each other.

Of the internal construction of the molecules which result from the union of atoms, it has been shown that we have some reason to believe that a certain degree of knowledge has been attained. Further information seems likely to result from the more careful attention which is now being given to the interrelation of chemical constitution and physical properties. The discoveries which have resulted from the careful study of the action of certain compounds on polarised light, encourages the belief that an equally careful investigation of the refractivity and dispersive power, of the electric conductivity, the viscosity, the specific volume, and the specific heat of pure substances of known composition may help in the further elaboration of those ideas of constitution which, imperfectly expressed in current chemical formulæ, have been derived from the observation of the modes of formation and of decomposition of compounds chiefly of one element, carbon. Valuable pioneering work of this kind has been already accomplished by Gladstone and by Brühl, by Hermann Kopp and by Thorpe, by Ostwald, Kohlrausch, and others. In the future one lesson derived from the past will doubtless be always borne in mind. The serious influence of small quantities of other substances in the materials which are the subject of experiment is now recognised, and the labour of physical measurements will surely in future be expended only upon substances which have been purified with the most scrupulous care, or of which the composition is accurately known.

But the exchange of the past tense for the future

is a sign that the story is drawing to a close. No Englishman, however, will consider the account complete without some attempt to form an estimate of the share which has been contributed to the progress of chemistry by his own countrymen. It is sometimes said that England has fallen behind in the race, and British chemists are reproached with inactivity, indolence, ignorance, and neglect. The days of Davy and Faraday are long past. "Those suns are set," the voice of dejection may be sometimes heard to exclaim, and

"All that we have left is empty talk
Of old achievements, and despair of new."

How far such assertions have any foundation in fact, the reader of this little volume may judge for himself; or if he desires categorical assurance, let him glance through the *Philosophical Transactions of the Royal Society* and the *Transactions of the Chemical Society* for the last thirty or forty years. In those volumes he will find proof that the chemists of Britain have not been negligent of the traditions which have come down to them from the famous days of old. If Dalton with his Atomic Theory laid the foundation of all the ideas of more recent times, the superstructure has been raised and adorned by the work and writings of Graham and Faraday, of Williamson and Frankland, of Odling and Gladstone, in friendly rivalry with their contemporaries in France and Germany.

If the discoveries of elements are to be enumerated, we can boast not only of oxygen and of potassium and sodium, but of thallium, one of the earliest and most remarkable trophies won by the spectroscope, and the whole of the new and strange companions of argon, while the principle of periodicity among the atomic weights was beyond question first enunciated by an Englishman. And if, unfortunately, it must be admitted that the cultivation of "organic" chemistry was pursued with but a languid interest for many years in England, the researches of Perkin alone, by their number, their variety, and their importance, go far towards making up for the deficiencies of others. This, however, can no longer be said, and English chemists can point with justifiable pride to the annual volume of *Transactions* issued by the Chemical Society, which, for excellence and quantity of matter, will bear comparison with the proceedings of any other chemical society in the world.

In the ancient universities of Great Britain, where chemistry has not flourished with the vigour shown by the older studies, the spirit of mediævalism is no longer wholly predominant. We may therefore look forward hopefully to the day, not far distant, when Science and Letters, no longer fierce competitors for academic vantage, may walk hand in hand, each conscious of her own dignity, but ready to yield to the other her due share of honour.

IMPORTANT EVENTS

ARRANGED IN CHRONOLOGICAL ORDER

Jean Baptiste Dumas born	1800
Friedrich Wöhler born	1800
Electrolytic decomposition of water by Nicholson and Carlisle	1800
Justus Liebig born	1803
Joseph Priestley (born 1733) died	1804
Thomas Graham born	1805
J. B. Richter (born 1762) died	1807
Atomic Theory of Dalton, published by Thomas Thomson	1807
Isolation of potassium and sodium	1807
Auguste Laurent born	1807
Henry Cavendish (born 1731) died	1810
Elementary nature of chlorine established	1810
Hypothesis of Avogadro	1811
Jean Servais Stas born	1813
Charles Gerhardt born	1816
Adolph Wurtz born	1817
Hermann Kopp born	1817
Jean Charles Galissard de Marignac born	1817
James Prescott Joule born	1818
Hermann Kolbe born	1818
August Wilhelm Hofmann born	1818
Law of Dulong and Petit	1819
Mitscherlich's first work on isomorphism	1819

Claude Louis Berthollet (born 1748) died	1822
Louis Pasteur born	1822
Faraday's first experiments on liquefaction of gases	1823
Berzelius' electro-chemical theory	1827
Wöhler's synthesis of urea	1828
Humphry Davy (born 1778) died	1829
William Hyde Wollaston (born 1766) died	1829
August Kekulé born	1829
Julius Lothar Meyer born	1830
Graham's law of gaseous diffusion	1831
Faraday's work in electricity begun	1831
British Association for the Advancement of Science founded	1831
Liebig and Wöhler on the "Radical of Benzoic Acid"	1832
Graham on arseniates and phosphates (recognition of basicity of acids)	1833
Faraday's first law of electro-chemical decomposition	1834
Dumas' discovery of chlorine substitution	1834
Carbon dioxide solidified by Thilorier	1835
Laurent's theory of nuclei used by Gmelin	1836
Dumas' theory of types	1839
Bunsen's discovery of cacodyl	1841
Chemical Society of London founded	1841
Homologous series recognised by Schiel	1842
Mechanical equivalent of heat determined by Joule	1842
John Dalton (born 1766) died	1844
Racemic acid dissected by Pasteur	1845
Synthesis of acetic acid by Kolbe	1845
College of Chemistry, London, founded	1845
Dissociation of water by heat (W. R. Grove)	1846
Frankland's discovery of ethyl	1848
Jöns Jakob Berzelius (born 1779) died	1848
Frankland's discovery of zinc-ethyl	1849
Wurtz's discovery of compound ammonias	1849

IMPORTANT EVENTS

Hofmann's synthetical formation of compound ammonias	1849
Louis Joseph Gay-Lussac (born 1778) died	1850
Constitution of ether established by Williamson	1850
Water-type proposed by Williamson	1851
Principle of "atomicity" recognised by Frankland	1852
Auguste Laurent died	1853
Law of Avogadro applied by Gerhardt	1853
Charles Gerhardt died	1856
Perkin discovers "Mauve"	1856
Clausius' theory of electrolysis	1857
Dissociation studied by Deville	1857
Linkage of atoms recognised by A. S. Couper	1858
Synthesis of acetylene (Berthelot)	1859
Spectrum analysis introduced by Bunsen and Kirchoff	1859
Pasteur's work on fermentation begun	1861
Eilhert Mitscherlich (born 1794) died	1863
Andrews' experiments on liquefaction of gases begun	1863
Atomicity applied to the explanation of isomerism by Crum Brown	1864
Newland's "Law of Octaves"	1864
Sprengel's mercury pump invented	1864
Kekulé's formula for benzene	1865
Bunsen's gas-burner invented	1866
Michael Faraday (born 1791) died	1867
German Chemical Society founded	1867
Synthesis of alizarin (Graebe and Liebermann, Perkin)	1868
Thomas Graham died	1869
Mendeléeff's first table of the elements	1869
Lothar Meyer's periodic curve	1870
Cannizzaro's Faraday Lecture	1872
Justus Liebig died	1873
Theory of stereo-isomerism (Le Bel and Van't Hoff)	1875
Liquefaction of oxygen (Pictet and Cailletet)	1877
Society of Chemical Industry founded	1881

Friedrich Wöhler died	1882
Hermann Kolbe died	1884
Jean Baptiste Dumas died	1884
Adolph Wurtz died	1884
Tautomerism or desmotropy recognised (Laar)	1885
Emil Fischer's synthesis of sugars begun	1885
Gas theory of solutions (Van't Hoff)	1887
Theory of free ions (Arrhenius)	1887
James Prescott Joule died	1889
Jean Servais Stas died	1891
August Wilhelm Hofmann died	1892
Hermann Kopp died	1892
Discovery of argon (Rayleigh and Ramsay)	1894
Discovery of terrestrial helium (Ramsay)	1894
Jean Charles Galissard de Marignac died	1894
Louis Pasteur died	1895
Julius Lothar Meyer died	1895
Critical temperature and boiling point of hydrogen determined by Olszewski	1895
August Kekulé died	1896
Liquefaction of hydrogen in quantity (Dewar)	1898

INDEX OF SUBJECTS

ALIZARIN from madder, 162
Allotropes, 25
American Chemical Society, 16
Ammonia type recognised, 119
Ammonium theory, 118
Anhydrides, formation of, 204
Argon, 52, 59
—— companions of, 57
Aromatic compounds, 138
Asymmetric carbon, 193, 196, 201
—— compounds, 188
Atomic theory, 60
—— weights, numerical relations of, 83
—— —— rectified, 60
Atomicity or equivalence, 127
Avogadro's hypothesis, 62, 70, 72

BASES, organic, Berzelius' theory of, 116
—— Hofmann's theory of, 119
—— Liebig's theory of, 117
—— Wurtz's theory of, 117
Benzene and its homologues, 137
Benzol discovered, 136
Benzoyl, compounds of, 111
British Association, 16
—— chemists defended, 265

CARBON compounds, 146
Cavendish on Air, 54
Chemical affinity, 209
—— elements, 37
—— Society of Berlin, 16

Chemical Society of London, 16
—— —— of Paris, 16
—— types, 66, 109
Clausius' theory of electrolysis, 225
Colouring matters, constitution of, 165
Combining weight of oxygen, 80, 82
Compound radicles, 14
Condensed types, 124
Conditions of chemical action, 259
Constitution of chemical compounds, 118
Constitutional formula, 181
Continuity of gaseous and liquid states of matter, 243
Copulated compounds, 122
Critical points, 246
Cyanogen, a compound radicle, 14, 112

DALTON'S Atomic Theory, 60
Dissociation, 34, 224
—— ionic, 224

ELECTRICITY and chemical affinity, 209
Electro-chemical theory of Berzelius, 210
—— —— of Davy, 210
Electrolysis, laws of, 211
   „   phenomena of, 214

INDEX OF SUBJECTS

Electrolytes, ionic, dissociation of, 224
Elements, 6, 24, 37, 39
—— Aristotelian, four, 38
—— classified, 83
—— distribution of, 37
—— positive and negative, 10
—— recognition of, 37
Endothermic compounds, 24, 32
Energy, 17, 18, 21
Enzymes, 175
Ether, constitution of, 64
Ethyl, compounds of, 111
Explosives, 168

FARADAY'S Laws of Electrolysis, 211
Fatty compounds, 138
Fermentation, alcoholic, 171
—— butyric, 174
—— lactic, 174
—— Liebig's theory of, 173
Fluorine, 50, 51, 52
Fraunhofer's lines, 43, 49
Freezing points of solutions, 217

GAS and vapour defined, 246
Gases, liquefaction of, 238
Genesis of the chemical elements, 104
Gerhardt's types, 125
Germanium identified with eka-silicon, 99
Graphic formulæ of Crum Brown, 134
—— —— of Couper, 134
—— —— of Kekulé, 134

HEAT, mechanical equivalent of, 22
Heat of neutralisation of acids, 231
Helium, 57, 59
Hemihedral crystals, 183

Homologous series, 113
Hydrochloric acid type, 123
Hydrogen liquefied, 248, 255
Hydrogen liquid, properties of, 256
Hydrogen type, 123

INDESTRUCTIBILITY of energy, 17
Indestructibility of matter, 5

KAKODYL, a compound radicle, 112
Kekulé's benzene formula, 140
Kinetic theory of gases, 222
Krypton, 57, 59

LACTONES, formation of, 204
Law of Avogadro, 62, 70, 72
—— of Dulong and Petit, 73
—— of octaves, 92
—— periodic, 88
Laws of Electrolysis, 211
Laurent's chemical method, 114
—— theory of nuclei, 114
Linking of atoms, 108
—— —— Kekulé on, 130
Liquefaction of gases, 238

MAGENTA discovered, 164
Mass, action of, 259
Matter and energy, 17
Mauve discovered, 163
Maximum work, 31
Mixed types, 123
Medicinal agents, synthetical, 167
Mendeléeff's eka-boron, &c., 98
—— table of elements, 97
Metalepsy, 65
Metargon, 57, 59
Meyer's curve, 96
Moisture, influence of on combination, 237
Molecules, Kelvin's estimate of size, 105

INDEX OF SUBJECTS

NEON, 57, 59
Nitrogen, density of, 53
Nuclei, Laurent's theory of, 114

OPTICALLY active liquids, 181
Organic chemistry defined, 144 *et seq.*
—— compounds defined, 144
Osmotic pressure, 220
Oxygen liquefied, 247

PERIODIC Law, 88
—— —— cause of, 103
Pharmaceutical Society, 16
Physical Society, 16
Polarised light, 181
Principle of maximum work, 31
Prothyl, 104
Prout's hypothesis, 84

RADICALS or radicles, 110, 112
Residual valency, 198
Residues, 67, 112
Royal Society, 2, 16
Royal Society of Edinburgh, 16

SALTS, haloid and amphid, 11
Semi-permeable membranes, 220
Société Chimique de Paris, 16
Society of Chemical Industry, 16
Solutions, gas theory of, 222
Solutions, properties of, 219
Space formulæ, 181
Spectrum analysis, 40
Spectrum of sunlight, 41
Stereo-chemistry, 181, 189
Substitution, 14, 65
Synthesis of carbon compounds, 149
Synthetical chemistry, 144

THERMO-CHEMISTRY, 27
Tria prima, 38

UNITARY system of formulæ, 215

VAPOUR pressures of solutions, 217
Valency, 108

WATER type recognised, 120
Williamson's theory of ether, 226

ZERO, absolute, 257

INDEX OF PERSONS

ALTHEN, Jean, 162
Andrews, 27, 28, 30, 242, 243
Arrhenius, 224
Avogadro, 62

BABBAGE, 16
Baeyer, von, 198, 204
Baker, W. H. B., 237
Bel, Le, 193
Berthelot, 30, 31, 124, 147, 262
Berthollet, 3, 259
Berzelius, 3, 10, 11, 66, 77, 109, 116, 210
Biot, 181
Blagden, 217
Boisbaudran, De, 41, 88
Boyle, 3, 18, 38
Brown, Crum, 134
Brühl, 264
Buchner, E., 179
Bunsen, 40, 112, 262

CAILLETET, 247, 249
Cannizzaro, 75
Carnelley, 103
Caro, 162
Cavendish, 54, 55, 209
Chancourtois, De, 88
Clarke, F. W., 82, 83
Clausius, 223, 225
Cooke, J. P., 82
Coppet, De, 217
Couper, A. S., 133
Crookes, 40, 102, 104

DALTON, 3, 7, 18, 60, 77, 189
Daniell, 11, 214, 215
Davy, 3, 9, 16, 17, 40, 210, 215, 232, 240
Deville, 34
Dewar, 249
Dixon, H. B., 236
Döbereiner, 85
Dulong, 26
Dulong and Petit, 72
Dumas, 14, 15, 65, 66, 67, 79, 85, 109, 122, 148

EWING, 254

FARADAY, 10, 11, 16, 136, 211, 240
Favre and Silbermann, 26, 30
Fittig and Tollens, 137
Foster, G. C., 132
Frankland, 111, 126, 135
Fraunhofer, 43, 49

GALVANI, 209
Gautier, 59
Gay-Lussac, 3, 12, 14, 61, 65
Gerhardt, 62, 63, 64, 68, 115, 125, 146, 154, 215
Gibbs, Willard, 36
Gladstone, 263, 264
Gmelin, 114, 146, 190
Graebe and Liebermann, 162
Graham, 11, 124
Griess, 165
Grotthus, 228

INDEX OF PERSONS

Grove, 34
Guldberg and Waage, 263
Guthrie, 217
Guye, 205

HAMPSON, 253
Harcourt and Esson, 262
Herschel, J., 44
Hess, 28, 30
Hill, A. C., 178
Hofmann, 71, 118
Hoff, Van't, 193, 195, 221, 222
Horstmann, 36

JAPP, 129, 143, 155
Jenner, 180
Joule, 18, 22, 23, 223, 252

KEKULÉ, 123, 129, 138, 146, 195
Kelvin, 105, 107, 252
Kirchhoff, 40
Kohlrausch, 229, 264
Kolbe, 123, 147
Kopp, 75
Körner, 142
Krönig, 223

LARMOR, 107
Lapparent, 88
Laurent, 113
Lavoisier, 1, 10, 12, 18, 26
Liebig, 11, 12, 109, 145, 173, 177
Liebig and Wöhler, 14, 110, 118
Linde, 253
Lister, 167
Lockyer, 57, 104

MALLET, 78
Mansfield, 136
Marggraff, 39
Marignac, 36, 77
Melsens, 149

Mendeléeff, 93, 96, 98
Meyer, L., 94
Miller, W. A., 44
Mitscherlich, 136
Moissan, 39, 52
Monge and Clouet, 239
Morley, 81

NAUMANN, 36
Newlands, J. A. R., 89, 91, 92
Newton, 17, 41
Nicholson and Carlisle, 9, 209
Nilson, 41
Northmore, 239

ODLING, 71, 89
Olszewski, 248

PASTEUR, 171, 180, 184
Pelouze, 77, 168
Perkin, 162, 164, 266
Perkin and Duppa, 158
Petit and Dulong, 72
Pfeffer, 221
Pictet, 247
Prout, 78, 83
Provostaye, De la, 184

RAMSAY, 55, 56
Ramsay and Travers, 57
Raoult, 217
Rayleigh, 53, 55, 82, 223
Regnault, 35, 75, 82
Reich and Richter, 40
Reynolds, O., 23
Rüdorff, 217
Rumford, 18

SCHEELE, 39
Schiel, 113
Schwann, 173
Scott, Alex., 81
Siemens, 253
Solvay, 253

Stas, 67, 77
Swan, 46

THÉNARD, 12
Thilorier, 241
Thomsen, Julius, 30, 33, 231
Thomson, W. *See* Kelvin
Thorpe, 264
Tilden and Marshall, 207
Tour, De la, C., 173, 239

VOLTA, 209

WALDEN, 207
Walker, J. W., 206
Waterston, 223
Williamson, 64, 120, 123, 226
Wislicenus, 192, 202
Wöhler, 39, 147
Wollaston, 43, 77, 190
Wroblewski, 248
Wunderlich, 200
Wurtz, 116, 124

ZININ, 137

THE END

Printed by BALLANTYNE, HANSON & CO.
Edinburgh & London

www.ingramcontent.com/pod-product-compliance
Lightning Source LLC
Chambersburg PA
CBHW032108230426
43672CB00009B/1671